UNORTHODOX

40
DISRUPTIVE
THOUGHTS
THAT
CHALLENGE
CONVENTIONAL
MINDSETS

MARTIJN VAN TILBORGH

For foreign and subsidiary rights, contact the author.

Cover & interior design by Joe De Leon of DeLeon Design
Cover photo by Andrew van Tilborgh

ISBN: 978-1-962401-24-1   1 2 3 4 5 6 7 8 9 10

Printed in the United States of America

UNORTHODOX

40
DISRUPTIVE
THOUGHTS
THAT
CHALLENGE
CONVENTIONAL
MINDSETS

BY SCANNING
THE QR CODE
BELOW YOU'LL
BE ABLE TO
ACTIVATE A
40-DAY VIDEO
SERIES THAT
ACCOMPANIES
THIS BOOK.
WE'LL TEXT
YOU A VIDEO
THAT EXPLAINS
THE PROCESS
INSTANTLY
ONCE YOU SCAN.

SCAN CODE TO ENTER THE →   UNORTHODOX 40-DAY JOURNEY

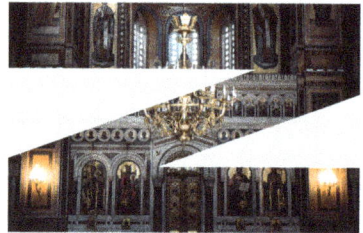

ACKNOWLEDGMENTS

I want to give special thanks to Sam Chand, a trusted mentor and friend. Sam—thank you for trusting me as your business partner and allowing me to be part of your world in co-creating the AVAIL brand. I cherish your brilliance and credit much of my success to you!

UNORTHODOX

What if the very idea of a "comfort zone" is the greatest adversary of growth? What if the safety zone, the tried-and-true business strategies, and the rinse-and-repeat formulas that have brought you some success are actually the enemy of your future?

The truth is no one will remember the things you did that worked. They will remember what you did that no one else would do. What would it take for you to be an audacious dreamer, undeterred by the risk of an enormous vision?

Unorthodox is not a gentle nudge but a clarion call to awaken the disruptive leader within you, the one who finds solace—and maybe even thrill—in the wilderness of challenge and change.

"Conventional" must be eliminated from our business vernacular. It no longer has a place in the vocabulary of anyone who wishes to walk ahead of the pack. Convention, in a sense, is the assassin of impact.

To be conventional is to follow the map; to be unorthodox is to draw your own. To be conventional is to use a key to unlock a door; to be unorthodox is to pick the lock. To be conventional whispers, "This is what has always worked;" to be unorthodox declares, "There's a better way."

Through forty thought-provoking reflections, this book is a deep dive into the heart of what it means to lead with the deep conviction that drives all revolutionary leaders: leadership is a continuous pursuit of the extraordinary in the face of the ordinary. It is a lifestyle of healthy rebellion against the status quo, an obstinate pursuit of "different", and an unmalleable expectation to stand out from the crowd and make waves that will change the world.

Throw out your predictable programs and step into the arena of unorthodox leadership. God uses singular (and unlikely!) voices to capture the attention of an entire nation—and sometimes—the world. There are countless people waiting to hear from those who speak louder than the rest, who are so unorthodox in their thinking that they know—without a doubt—that it is God's maverick spirit working in them and through them simply because of their shameless unorthodoxy.

I don't know if you've noticed, but God is pretty unorthodox. A leader who is humble and courageous enough to allow God to fashion him into His unorthodox image will spread the gospel faster than leaders who choose the path most traveled, simply because they are leading the way Christ leads His people. Your unique imprint in God's Kingdom will spread like wildfire and people will notice. They will know there is something different about you. Like a moth to the flame, they too will begin to brave the Wild West, following your lead, creating a ministry of their own that will shake the very foundations of "acceptable".

Faith grows in tandem with pressure. Leaders can find strange comfort in the constant stretching of their capacity. The way you lead your organization or ministry should be a magnet for souls who are stuck in the same narrative and the mundane rhythms of work. The way you lead should be a crucible of divine challenge that becomes your battle cry, one that doesn't just tickle the ears, but marks the heart for eternal purpose.

Don't settle for business as usual.

Step outside of the shadows of conformity, defy the norm, and take your stand as the pioneer of the unorthodox!

ONE

THE WILDERNESS AS YOUR COMFORT ZONE

MANY DREAM about becoming an influential leader—to change the world. Then, when you become a leader. . . . reality sets in.

The truth is, fulfilling the dream that God has given you is hard. Once you have reached a level of success, people around you may look at you and think, "You have it so easy!" Have you ever heard that before?

I get it. I was there once myself, marveling at the guys who "made it". Those who were leading organizations with big budgets where money didn't seem to be an issue and where everything they undertook seemed to be successful.

Somehow, I came to believe the lie that once you become one of "those guys", you don't need as much faith to remain successful. In my mind, I would no longer be chasing after the dream. I would just announce my arrival by reclining, kicking my feet up, sipping on my coffee, and eating bonbons.

Fast forward, and now I have come to be "one of those guys". . . and to the harsh realization that eating bonbons means saying goodbye to success.

More success will require more faith and more responsibility.

Yes, I know it sounds counterintuitive, but I promise you—it's true.

The pursuit of God's potential in your life will demand a greater level of faith with every success you experience.

And here I was, thinking that I only needed faith in the wilderness!

Yet, the promised land is where your faith is truly put to the test, so much so that going back to the wilderness seems like an appealing option.

Sure, right after you leave "Egypt", the wilderness is a scary place. It feels unfamiliar, unpredictable, and dangerous.

Yet after being there for a while, it actually becomes familiar to you. It's not so bad after all. In fact, the wilderness becomes not only familiar, but attractive. Predictable even!

That's because familiarity demands less responsibility. All we have to do is follow the leader. True, there isn't much abundance to go around, but come early morning, there is always food.

Before you know it, you have made a home in a place that looks and feels comfy but is actually stuffy and even hostile. Don't be fooled!

Once you cross that river Jordan, these dynamics will change instantly. The things you could count on in the wilderness are no longer there.

Said another way—you are on your own! Or so it feels. God will still take care of you, but it requires a different kind of faith.

Going on autopilot isn't an option anymore. There isn't a "standard process" we can follow. The strategy that gives us victory over "Jericho" kicks our butts in "Ai".

You have to stay sharp in your promised land in order for your winning streak to continue.

You are now burdened with the responsibility to lead well, because failing to do so may get you (and others) hurt.

The promised land can wear you out and burn you out to the point where you will begin to desire the wilderness.

This is difficult to comprehend if you have not yet made it to your promised land. Talk to any promised land resident, and they will tell you that fatigue is plentiful there. Yet, others won't see it, because they will be too focused on being you—"that guy".

Today I want to encourage you that fatigue is expected. In fact, if you are fatigued, you are doing something right. You are leading well. Most importantly, you are not alone.

Press on, push through it, and whatever you do, do not give up.

It's not called the promised land for nothing. In fact, there are two promises there waiting for you—the promise of pressure and the promise of plenty.

Embrace the pressure, reap plenty.

THE PURSUIT OF GOD'S POTENTIAL IN YOUR LIFE WILL DEMAND A GREATER LEVEL OF FAITH WITH EVERY SUCCESS YOU EXPERIENCE.

YOU JUST DON'T HAVE WHAT IT TAKES!

3

EVERY DAY, I get to talk to people who have desires, dreams, and visions for what they want to accomplish in their lives. Dreams big enough to not only transform their own lives, but the lives of the people around them.

Here's the challenge, though.

These people that I talk about (unfortunately) do NOT have what it takes! What they "carry" is simply NOT GOOD ENOUGH to "get the job done." There is just too much of a discrepancy between their abilities and where God wants to take them in life.

Yes, I know, these are quite depressing statements.

But let me explain.

Remember the story in Scripture where Jesus told his disciples to feed the five thousand people who had been listening to Him all day long?

They were hungry and needed to eat!

Well, the reality was that the disciples simply didn't have what it took to get that job done. Jesus's assignment was simply too big! Five loaves and two fishes weren't going to feed even a fraction of the crowd they were asked to feed.

Here's the reality: none of us have what it takes to "feed the multitudes" (whatever "feeding the multitudes" means for you). We're all in a place where we don't have enough resources (and I don't mean just money) at our disposal to accomplish everything that God is asking of us.

Hearing this, you may be tempted to not do anything at all. You may be thinking: I don't have what it takes, so why bother?

But here is the beauty of that story.

Jesus didn't focus on what He didn't have. Out of the many things He could have focused on, He focused on what He DID have. He simply did what He could do and started breaking what He knew was "not enough." He started with what He could start with, and that alone allowed the Father to multiply His efforts.

And that's when the miracle happened!

At the end of the story, all were fed. In fact, they packed twelve take-home baskets after it was all said and done.

So, I've made a decision. Instead of waiting for the perfect circumstances, I'm going to focus on what I do have and what I can do while trusting God to multiply my efforts. It's not about what you have; it's what you do with what you have!

Don't wait around for the perfect circumstances before doing anything.

You have the ability to transform the world around you.

Get started with what you have, and let God do the rest!

INSTEAD OF WAITING FOR THE PERFECT CIRCUMSTANCES, I'M GOING TO FOCUS ON WHAT I DO HAVE AND WHAT I CAN DO WHILE TRUSTING GOD TO MULTIPLY MY EFFORTS. IT'S NOT ABOUT WHAT YOU HAVE; IT'S WHAT YOU DO WITH WHAT YOU HAVE!

DON'T WAIT AROUND FOR THE PERFECT CIRCUMSTANCES BEFORE DOING ANYTHING. YOU HAVE THE ABILITY TO TRANSFORM THE WORLD AROUND YOU. GET STARTED WITH WHAT YOU HAVE, AND LET GOD DO THE REST!

YOU JUST DON'T HAVE WHAT IT TAKES!

3

THE
EVOLUTION
OF THEOLOGY

AS GOD'S KINGDOM IS REVEALED MORE AND MORE THROUGH- OUT THE AGES, WE START TO UNDER- STAND MORE AND MORE OF WHO GOD REALLY IS.

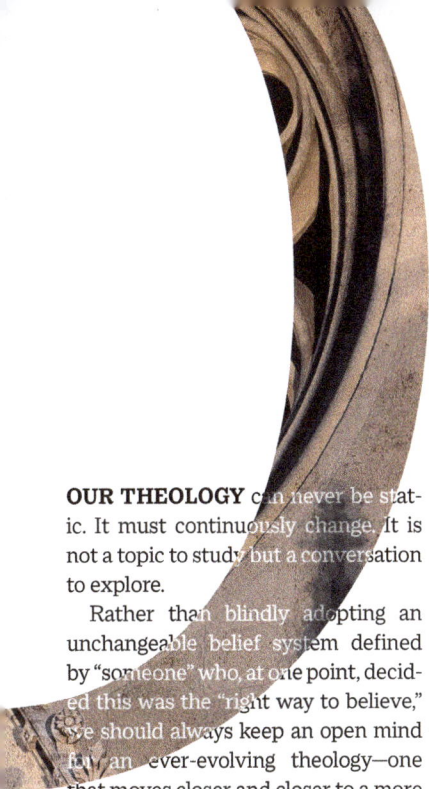

OUR THEOLOGY can never be static. It must continuously change. It is not a topic to study but a conversation to explore.

Rather than blindly adopting an unchangeable belief system defined by "someone" who, at one point, decided this was the "right way to believe," we should always keep an open mind for an ever-evolving theology—one that moves closer and closer to a more accurate understanding of who God really is.

Not so much because God changes His mind all the time, but rather because humanity (and creation as a whole) is on a journey to discover who He truly is.

Let me illustrate what I mean.

Abraham's theology (for example) was different from Moses's theology, which was different from Jesus's theology, which was different from Paul's theology, and so forth.

It appears that as God "travels" with humanity through time and history, He continues to adjust our perception of who He is to a more accurate understanding.

At the offset of Abraham's story, his "theology" allowed for the possibility of child sacrifice, something that was pretty common during the cultural milieu of that time of history. Abraham's belief system changed when God took him on a journey one day, which led him to alter his belief system about Him.

He no longer had to do what he believed God required of him.

God didn't change.

It was Abraham who changed!

Abraham changed his theology about who God truly was by gaining access to an insight (or revelation) he didn't have before.

By the time Moses was in charge, the doctrine of child sacrifice was no longer a common belief. The general consensus was that God no longer required such a thing. (Not that He ever did, to begin with).

Today, we can't even imagine such a thing ever existed. Our theology doesn't even come close to the theology of that time.

As God's kingdom is revealed more and more throughout the ages, we start to understand more and more of who God really is.

The greater the revelation of Him, the more it requires us to alter what we believe.

As I read through Scripture and study how God interacts with humanity through time, it appears that He gets both "closer" as well as "kinder" to us—again, not because He has changed but because our understanding of Him has changed.

As time passes, God seems to strip away all the things that we told ourselves we should do to please Him. Not just child sacrifice, like Abraham believed, but any sacrifice. Even the laws of Moses became irrelevant by the time Jesus appeared on the scene.

Perhaps there is very little we can do to "please Him."

Perhaps He is already pleased with us, regardless of what we "do" or "do not" do.

Could it be that this is what the gospel is all about?

Could it be that all of this is not as much about what we believe about Him but more about what He believes about us?

Because, if it is, well . . . I call that "Good News"!

COULD IT BE THAT THIS IS WHAT THE GOSPEL IS ALL ABOUT? COULD IT BE THAT ALL OF THIS IS NOT AS MUCH ABOUT WHAT WE BELIEVE ABOUT HIM BUT MORE ABOUT WHAT HE BELIEVES ABOUT US?

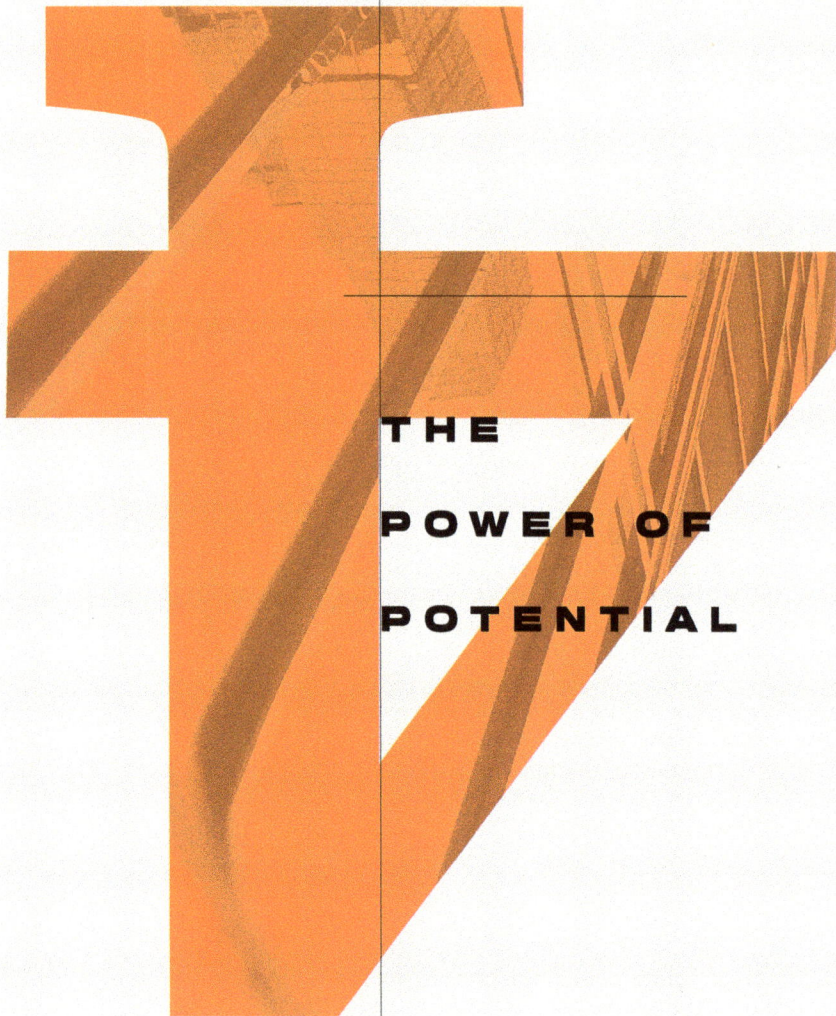

THE
POWER OF
POTENTIAL

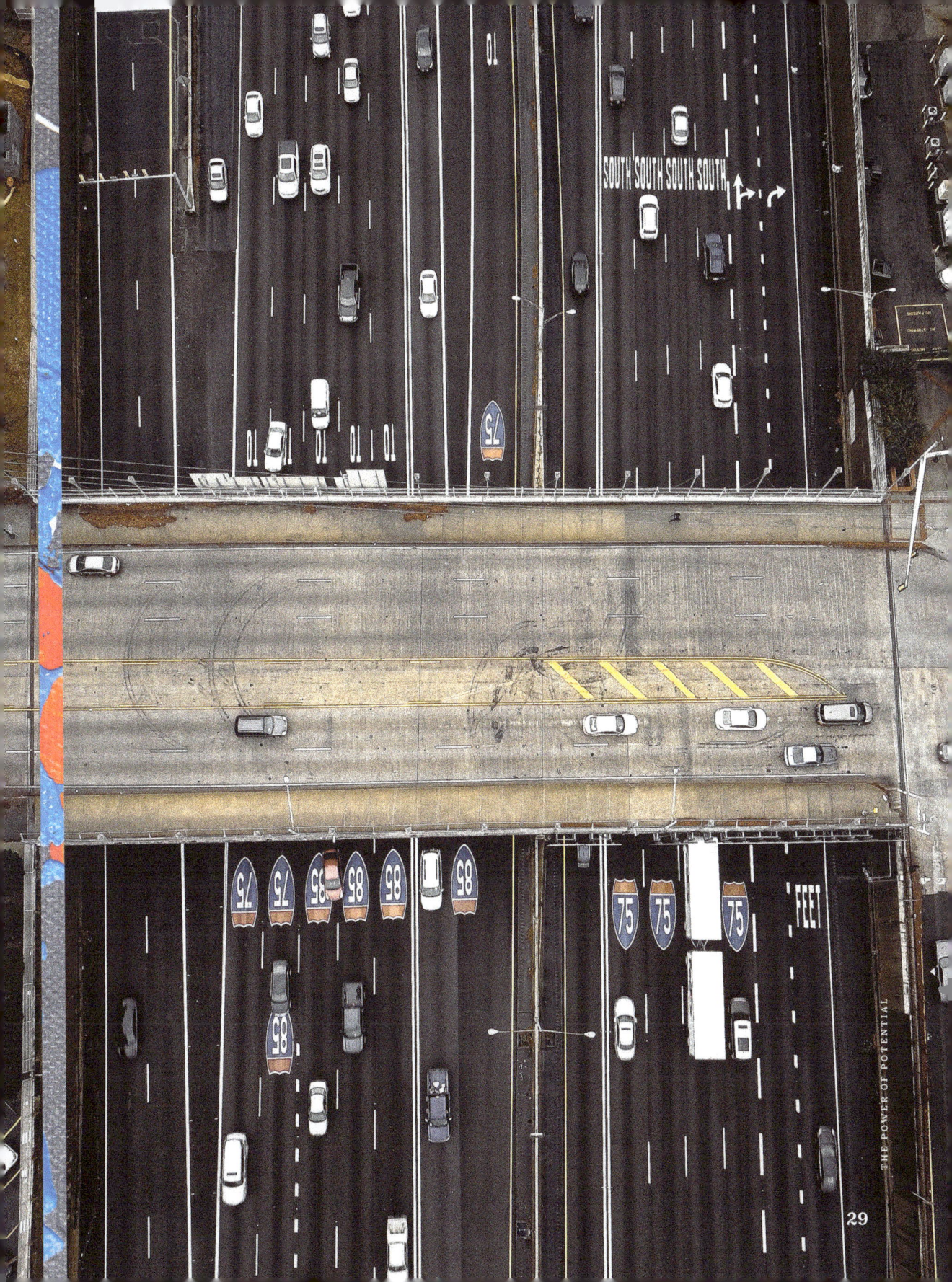

I'VE ALWAYS been intrigued by the story of Abraham—an ordinary man who grew up in the midst of a pagan society in Mesopotamia, a region now known as Iraq.

One could argue that Abraham was an unlikely candidate to be noticed by God. Yet God, in His unwavering desire to make us prosper, met Abraham in his idolatry to show him a greater reality of what his life could look like.

God had seen something in Abraham that he couldn't see in himself. Until that moment, Abraham had assumed a life of mediocrity.

Yet God's spoken words caused Abraham to see his life not just as it was but as it could be. This new reality gave Abraham the courage to uproot his family and embark on a journey that would revolutionize his future.

I think it could be tempting to look at Abraham and think, "Don't even think about comparing me to him. I could never accomplish the things he did. He left everything behind in pursuit of some ambiguous promise!"

I get it. It's easy to see Abraham through rose-colored glasses because that level of faith is hard to fathom. Surely, there was something remarkable and extraordinary about him from the start that made him the prime candidate to become the father of many nations.

You would be mistaken.

We are no different than Abraham. Abraham was pretty ordinary, just like us. Nothing extraordinary came out of him until God got His hands on him.

Just like God saw something in Abraham that he couldn't, He sees things in us that we can't see in ourselves—things that can become a reality if we have the courage to leave the old behind in pursuit of the land He wants to lead us to.

You see, God will never speak to our mediocre status quo. He will always speak to our potential future.

The dictionary defines potential as "having the capacity to become something in the future."

Potential is not what I have done but what I have not done and still can do.

Potential is not what I have but what I do not have and still can have.

Potential is not who I am but who I am not and still can be.

"Ordinary" is an asset, not a deficit.

God does not use men and women who are already superstars . . . because there is no such thing.

That should make you breathe a sigh of relief because that can only mean one thing—He has great plans for you!

HE HAS GREAT PLANS FOR YOU!

F
I
V
E

ARE YOU READING HIS "FIRST BIBLE"?

M

MOST OF US are familiar with the first book of the Bible, where God created the heavens and the earth. The story goes that God spoke all of creation into existence.

It was His WORD that created ALL THINGS.

Isaiah 55 later explains that God's WORD never returns void. It always prospers in the things for which it was sent.

Many years later, John puts it into his own words:

"In the beginning was the Word, and the Word was with God, and the Word was God. . . . Through him all things were made, and without Him nothing was made that has been made" (John 1:1-3, NIV).

Think about that for a minute and let it sink in.

If the "WORD = GOD" and the "WORD = ALL OF CREATION," then something of "GOD" is hidden (and found) in "ALL THINGS" that are created.

Perhaps that's why Isaiah continues his train of thought by explaining that "the mountains and the hills burst forth into singing" and that the "trees clap their hands" (Isaiah 55:12, author paraphrase).

God seems to have a special connection with ALL of creation (not just humans) to the point where even "the stones will cry out" (Luke 19:39, NIV).

So, where am I going with this?

For starters, all of this makes me wonder.

Could it be that sometimes we're looking for God in the wrong places? That maybe He's much bigger than we think? (Imagine that!)

Could it be that, at some level, God's very presence can be found in all things that were created? That He exists in places outside of our religious paradigms?

Could it be that we "miss God" because He's hiding in plain sight?

Could it be that some nonbelievers (who, by the way, were also created by His word) are sometimes more in tune with God's involvement in . . . well . . . everything that exists than us religious folks? Perhaps so much so that they find it easier to participate in God's "divine dance" with humanity and, really, all of creation?

Did God give us "a first Bible" when He created all things through His word (long before our current Bible was ever written)?

Here's my final question that I encourage you to ponder.

Does God ever really stop speaking to us?

"IN THE BEGINNING WAS THE WORD, AND THE WORD WAS WITH GOD, AND THE WORD WAS GOD. THROUGH HIM ALL THINGS WERE MADE, AND WITHOUT HIM NOTHING WAS MADE THAT HAS BEEN MADE."

ARE YOU READING HIS "FIRST BIBLE"?

COULD IT BE THAT SOMETIMES WE'RE LOOKING FOR GOD IN THE WRONG PLACES? THAT MAYBE HE'S MUCH BIGGER THAN WE THINK?

6

BAIT AND SWITCH CHRISTIANITY

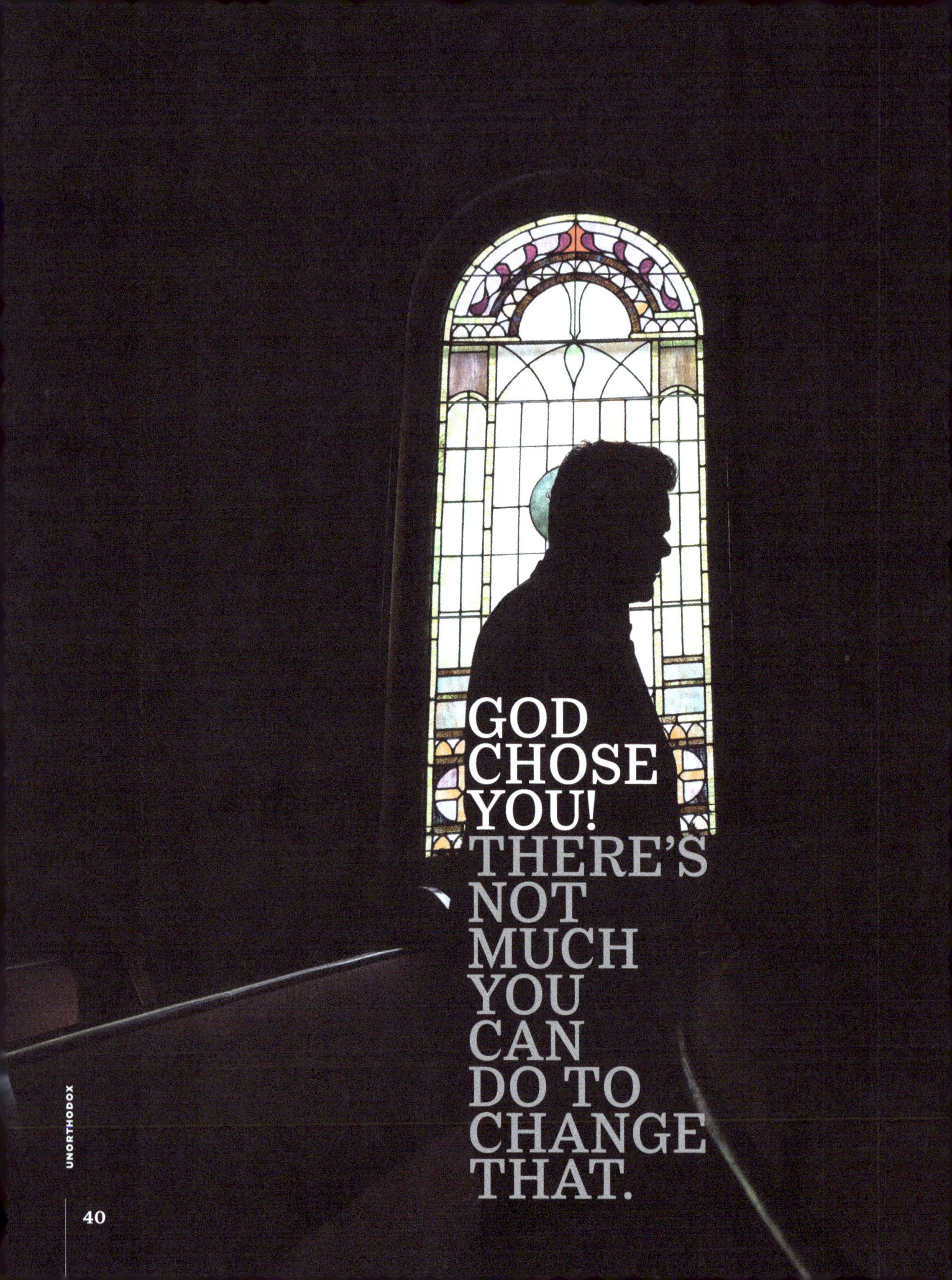

GOD CHOSE YOU! THERE'S NOT MUCH YOU CAN DO TO CHANGE THAT.

GROWING UP in church, I was always told that "the gospel is free."

It wasn't about "what you do" but all about "who you are" in God's eyes.

On the flip side, though, I quickly discovered that "who I was" wasn't good enough to "get to heaven."

After all, "my sinful nature deserved to die."

So, in order to escape "eternal death," I needed to DO something first!

Things like "Have faith," "Believe," or "Pray the magic prayer" because when you DO these things, you'll be okay.

Under the surface, there were questions, though:

How much faith is actually enough faith?

What if there are days when I don't have as much faith?

Will I still be fine?

And what is the shelf life of that "magic prayer"?

Is praying it one time enough?

Or should I pray it more often?

If so, how many times would be ideal?

You can see how some people may have a hard time dealing with these questions.

Then, I discovered a lot more "small print" in the "terms and conditions" that I failed to read when I signed up for all this.

Now that I was "in," I realized that there was something called "church attendance" because, after all, you're a Christian now.

That's what you do!

But how often is enough?

Well, weekly, of course, but if I was really serious about my faith, I should also find a connect group, come to the prayer meeting, and volunteer my time.

And what about my quiet time?

My prayer life?

My tithes and offerings?

The "strings" that came attached with that gift that was supposed to be FREE seemed to exponentially increase as soon as I "signed on that dotted line."

"Who I was" no longer seemed to be important. It was all about "what I did."

Before long, I, too, became one of those Old Testament Pharisees who ended up with 613 rules that came with "being chosen."

The bar for "being in" became higher and higher and more difficult to attain.

So much so that I started to wonder if that "gift from God" was truly free.

And whether or not this "good news" was actually "too good to be true"?

A friend of mine shared this question the other day:

Does grace "lower the bar" or "raise the bar" or "replace the bar"?

It's an incredible question to meditate on.

What's the answer?

Well, here's my conclusion:

It's the wrong question to ask!

The question assumes that there is a bar to reach while, in reality, there isn't one.

God chose you! There's not much you can do to change that.

BLOW
OFF
THE
LIP

EARLIER THIS YEAR, I found myself in a meeting with high-capacity (A-List) ministry leaders. There were about thirty of us in the room, and we were discussing various topics relating to leadership, the state of the church, and how to create a greater positive impact.

I don't exactly remember who made the comment, but I recall a statement was made that became the catalyst for a much larger conversation.

As we were talking about a wide variety of leadership topics, our conversation evolved into discussing "the future of the church."

In the midst of our dialogue, someone made the well-intended comment, "Our congregation will NEVER outgrow our pulpits!"

His point was that "we," as leaders, have a responsibility. We have to set a certain standard that our people can look up to. After all, "We don't want to be the bottleneck for their growth."

A shock of awe went through the room. This particular leader had not just articulated a profound "truth," but he had also been able to sum it up in just one concise sentence.

Before long, others started to chip into the conversation, reinforcing the "reality" that if we as preachers failed to set the right example, "our people would never reach their full potential."

On the surface, all of this sounded so good and right.

Yet, on a deeper level, I felt uneasy about where this discussion was going.

It was as if God were whispering in my ear:

Wow! You guys really think very highly of yourself to think that you are the ceiling for someone else's growth potential. Do you really think that all My goals and aspirations that I have for My people are conditioned by how you act as leaders? Believe Me, I'm smarter than that!

Wow, imagine that!

Sure, as leaders, we can play an important role in people's lives. And yes, there should be a standard that others can look up to, but to think that we are somehow the greatest among many is the wrong way to look at things.

To put it in the words of the greatest man who ever stood in the pulpit:

"Very truly I tell you, whoever believes in me will do the works I have been doing, and they will do even greater things than these" (John 14:12, NIV).

Let's stop taking ourselves too seriously.

As leaders, we just don't have that much power.

Instead of capping people's potential through our leadership, let's blow off the lid altogether!

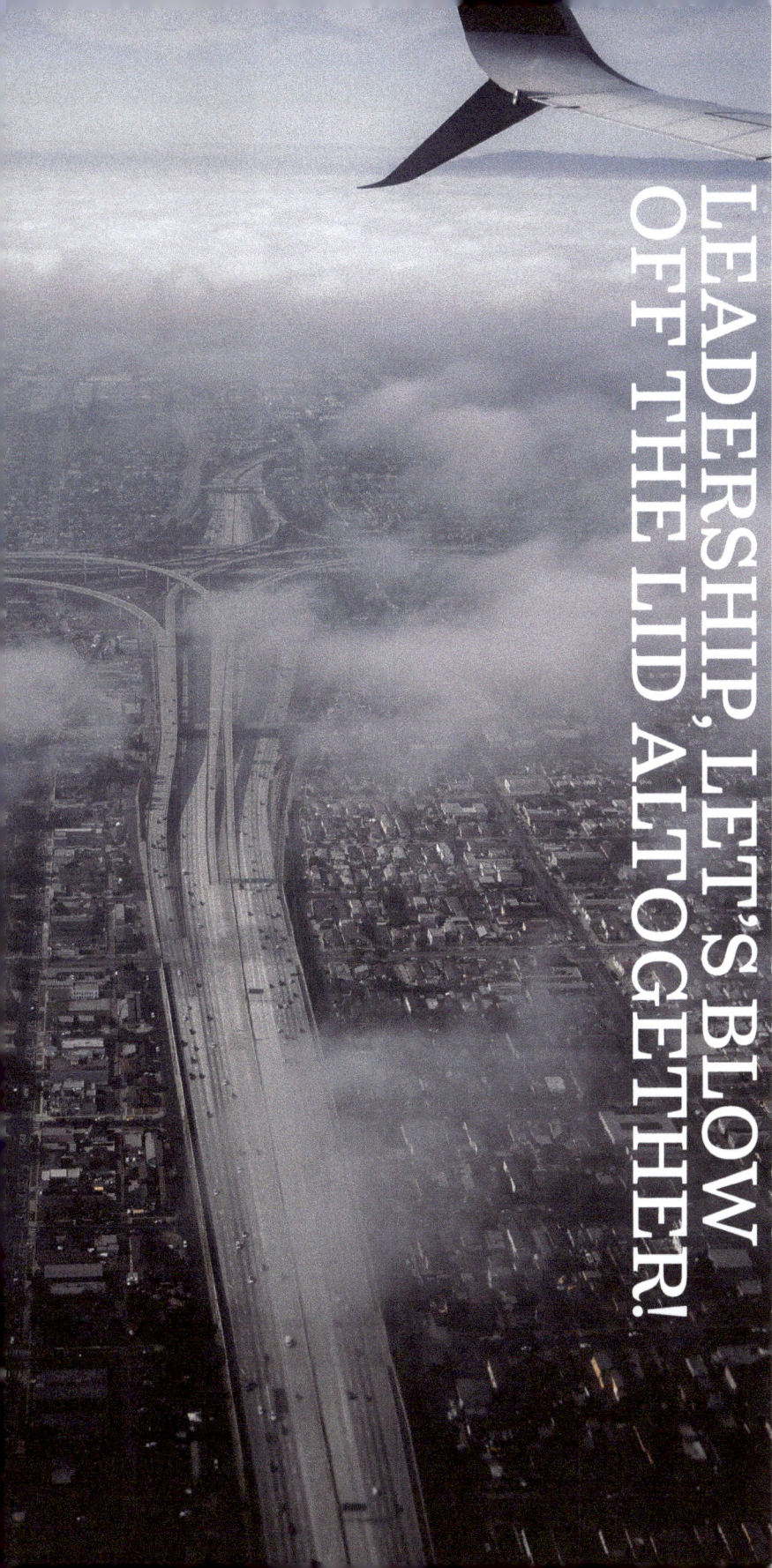

INSTEAD OF CAPPING PEOPLE'S POTENTIAL THROUGHOUR LEADERSHIP, LET'S BLOW OFF THE LID ALTOGETHER!

PEDALING HARDER TO MAINTAIN YOUR SPEED

EIGHT

UNORTHODOX

46

PEDALING HARDER TO MAINTAIN YOUR SPEED

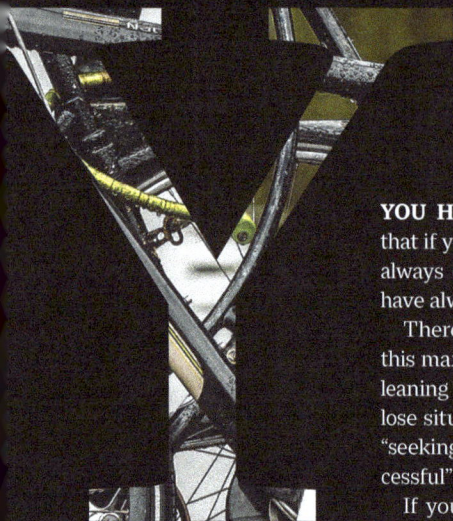

YOU HAVE probably heard it said that if you keep doing what you have always done, you will get what you have always gotten.

There are a lot of problems with this maxim. I would not recommend leaning into it. It presents a lose-lose situation for leaders in both the "seeking success" and "already successful" camps.

If you are struggling to find your way and far from success, you certainly do not want to keep doing what you have always done. So, that's a nail in the coffin.

If you are soaring and growing leaps and bounds, you will never soar higher if you keep doing what you have always done. Another nail in the coffin.

Either way, you're buried.

Pretty depressing, huh? Especially for anyone who believes that God wants more for us. It doesn't matter whether you are a business owner, industry leader, mother, student, or husband—I think you get the picture. Doing the same thing over and over again is never the answer.

However, putting this maxim into practice actually yields consequences even more damaging than that because if you just keep doing what you have always done, you will find—after time—that it takes more of doing the same to get what you have always gotten.

Are you getting that?

Repeating the same old tricks won't just cause you to coast; it will cause you to sink.

It's possible that what you are doing is actually a good thing. An effective thing. The "right" thing. There may be nothing inherently wrong with your method or approach. However, doing "the right thing" in the wrong season is counterproductive.

Many times, continuing to do the things that provided us with past successes will actually push us into a downward spiral of declining results.

It's the law of diminishing returns: the more you try to pour new wine into old wineskins, the greater the spill.

So, you have to pedal harder to maintain your speed.

Therefore, not only will simply doing what we have always done keep us from the bigger future God has in mind, but over time, it will prevent us from even maintaining what we have in the present.

Here's what I'd like to leave you with today.

God will never ask you to stay where you are. If you are in the same place as you were six months ago, a year ago, or five years ago, you can take it to the bank—God has already determined to give you a greater measure of input so that you can produce a greater measure of output.

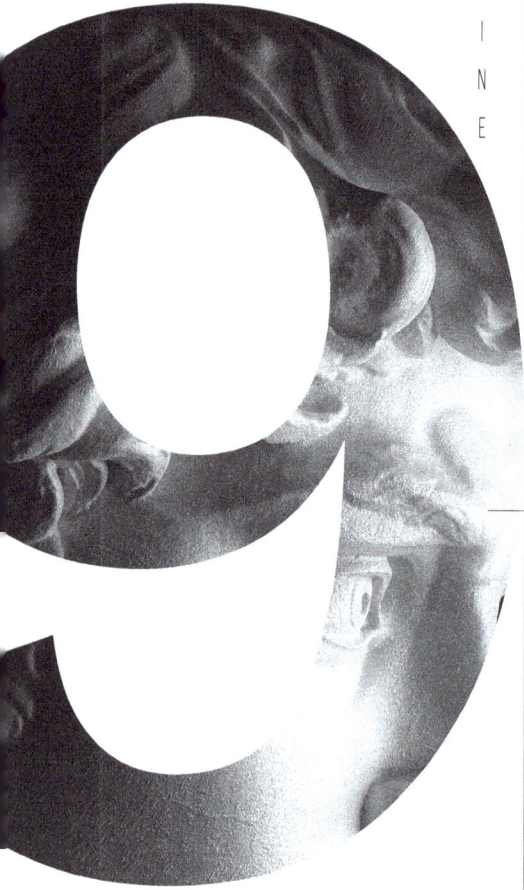

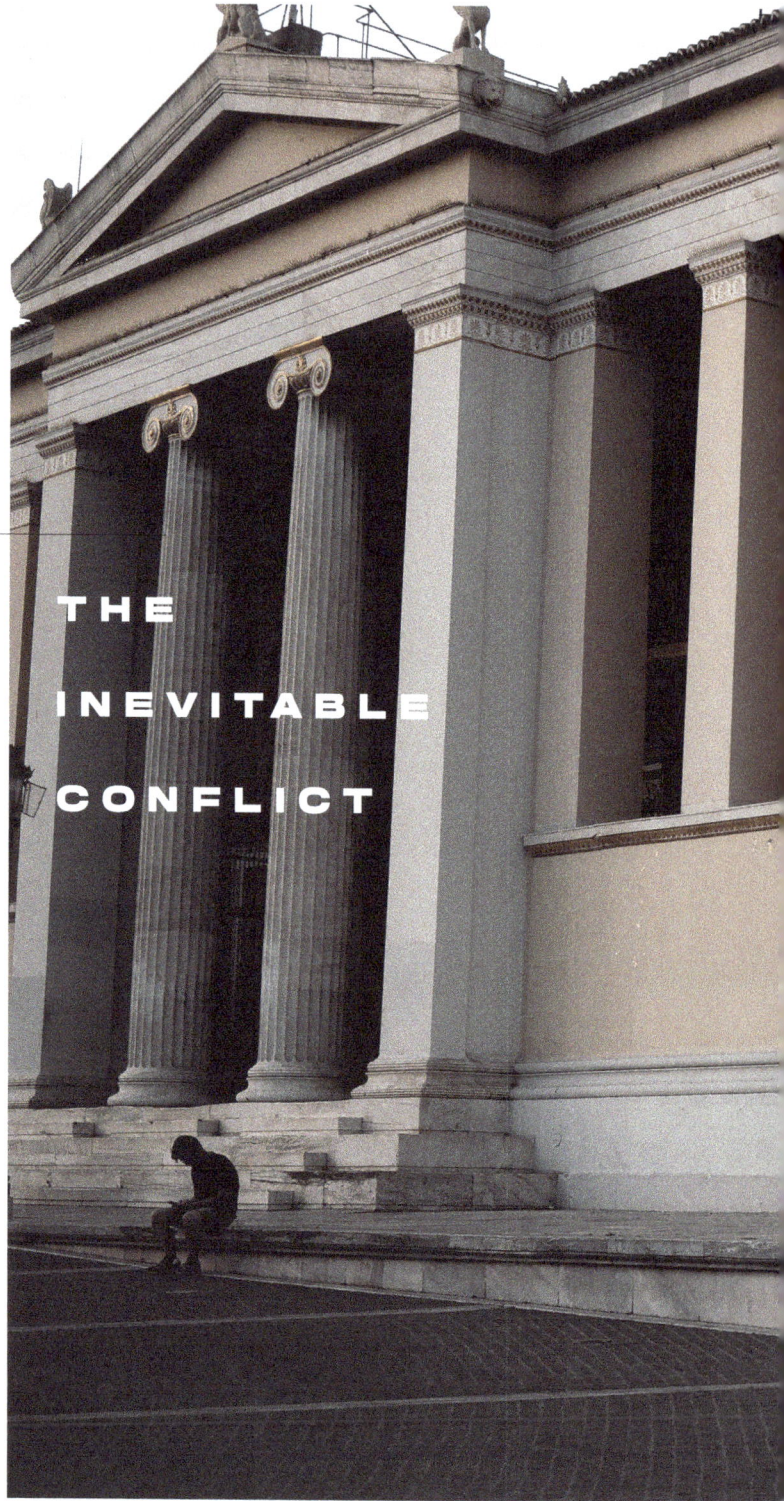

THE
INEVITABLE
CONFLICT

ACCORDING TO the wisest man who ever lived, there is a time for everything—including conflict. In Ecclesiastes 3:8 (KJV), Solomon wrote that there is "a time of war, and a time of peace."

Please note that this portion of scripture in the King James Version doesn't use the phrase "a time for war," but rather "a time of war." I'd like to unpack that a little more. A time for war would suggest that at some specified time, we must initiate and declare war, and on many occasions that may be true. But a time of war implies that we have no choice in whether or not it will occur. Our decision is what we are going to do when it inevitably breaks out.

I believe that this is where we are now in the church.

A time of conflict is upon us—an inevitable war between the old and the new.

Between the good and the better.

Between the church of the past, the church of today, and the church of tomorrow.

The only question is this: which side are you on?

I've chosen "tomorrow"! Are you with me?

As you may have noticed, many Christians are looking behind, hoping that we will return to "the ways things used to be." It's understandable. It is natural to grieve the past. We want the familiar. We were happy. We were comfortable. And in many ways, we were oblivious. There is no denying that we find ourselves at a pivotal moment in history.

The truth is, we can look to the future without anxiety and fear in the spirit of hope, great expectation, and delight in the new thing God is doing. After all, that's what Christ came for, right? To free us from fear of what's to come tomorrow and endear us to the great plans that He has for us?

God wants us to look up and ahead for what's to come, not down and back at what once was.

I understand this mindset is challenging to adopt. It may take time. That's okay—because moving on is never easy. There are few things more painful for a human than change. But, the future comes at a price. The odds may even be stacked against us. However, it's a conflict that is worth the risk because victory will push us deeper into the unfolding plan that God has for creation—to see His kingdom manifest on earth as it already is in heaven.

I'm neither advocating that you forget the past nor the present. Rather, I'm offering a bid for you to thank God for what they offered at their allotted time—a bigger harvest for the future.

THE TRUTH IS

WE CAN
LOOK TO
THE FUTURE
WITHOUT
ANXIETY
AND FEAR
IN THE
SPIRIT
OF HOPE,
GREAT
EXPECTA-
TION, AND
DELIGHT IN
THE NEW
THING GOD
IS DOING.

THE GREAT ATTENTION SHIFT

ACCORDING TO research, even the most committed families in our churches only show up 1.8 times every month.

That really sucks when you preach a six-week sermon series, and people are only there for "Episode" 2.

And 6.

As a consultant, I'm often asked about strategies on how to get people back in the pew week after week.

Sure, there are tons of gimmicky and manipulative marketing tricks that can be deployed to shame and guilt people back in their seats every Sunday.

But is this really the way we want to go?

In order to "fix" the issue, we need to understand the underlying problem. The real problem at hand is what I call "the great attention shift."

This is not something new. Attention shifts happen all the time, not just in church. In every industry and market, we experience waves of change as the attention of the people we're trying to serve shifts.

Shifts in attention make previous distribution models obsolete. We used to buy toys in stores; now, we buy them online. We used to go to restaurants for the convenience of not having to cook. Now, we're ordering food on an app from restaurants that specialize in delivery only. We used to shop at K-Mart, call a taxi for transport, and go to Blockbuster to rent a movie.

But guess what? The attention of the market has shifted!

The church is not exempt from attention shifts.

Instead of blaming our congregations for not showing up, we should ask ourselves what value we are offering to the people we're serving.

Are we giving a reason to trade their time for what we're offering weekly?

It's all about supply and demand.

You see, the market is always right. According to our target audience, the value we're offering is only worth 1.8 Sundays of their precious time.

Yet we continue to build systems and structures around the assumption that the model we used for the last fifty years is the model we're going to have until the end of days. We continue to invest our time, energy, and money based on the assumption that the distribution model of how we do church will remain the same.

Don't be fooled!

Let's take the log out of our own eyes and understand shifts in attention in order to redefine and reposition ourselves so we can better serve the people we've been called to serve.

THE BRIDGE BETWEEN

LACK AND ABUNDANCE

2 KINGS 4, we read about a widow who found herself and her family in a desperate situation. Her circumstances had led her onto a path where she accumulated a tremendous amount of debt. There simply wasn't a way out for her unless God intervened.

And He did!

The answer to her situation came through a simple question from Elisha: "Tell me, what do you have in your house?"

The question asked by the prophet implies that, even in the most desperate situations, there is something close at hand that is the answer to your problem. Elisha's question pushed her to identify the very thing that would become the vehicle of her deliverance.

It was a small jar of olive oil—something seemingly insignificant that became a weapon of war that would lead her to victory, favor, and incredible abundance.

The takeaway from this story was that the answer to her problem was not found externally.

Her situation was "fixed" through something she already possessed. Something seemingly small didn't just become the antidote to her problems; it became a source of abundance that would leave a legacy for her family.

See, small keys open big doors. This is kind of God's motto if you will. His glory shines brightest when He can take something that looks insignificant and produce something that we could never manufacture on our own. God doesn't need big things. He only needs small things—I think, smaller than we even realize.

Consider the story of Gideon in the book of Judges. Like many other rescuers in the Bible, Gideon was convinced God had the wrong person. There was no way he could lead his tiny little army into victory over the mighty Midianites, whose army was more than six times the Israelite army's size!

Nevertheless, God speaks that word that should change everything about the way we see lack and abundance: "Go in the strength you have." I think it's pretty safe to say Gideon didn't have a whole lot of that. But what he had was ENOUGH. God can work with enough because it is GOD who will accomplish immeasurable beyond what Gideon could ask, think, or imagine . . . and He did!

The moral of the story is that the bridge between lack and abundance is found in something you already own, not something outside of your reach!

The key is to hear "the voice of God" in your current circumstance that will allow you to leverage something you've already got to take you from lack to abundance. The kingdom of God is always within arm's reach.

The answer to your problem is always already in your possession.

HE CAN TAKE SOMETHING THAT LOOKS INSIGNIFICANT AND PRODUCE SOMETHING THAT WE COULD NEVER MANUFACTURE ON OUR OWN.

INNOVATION
VS.
ADAPTATION
VS.
OPTIMIZATION

INNOVATION VS. ADAPTATION VS. OPTIMIZATION

TRUE

INNOVATION ISN'T EASY. We often pretend to innovate, while in reality, we are merely adapting to new circumstances or optimizing within an existing structure.

While adaptation and optimization may create the illusion of innovation, we need to understand the differences in order to be effective as leaders.

Let's explore that difference:

Adaptation is reactive. It is a pivot in response to a change. When circumstances change, they force us to do something different. We can no longer do what we used to do. We simply adapt to what we call the "new normal" in order to survive in the new climate.

Oftentimes, this is just a different version of the same thing.

Optimization is slightly different than adaptation. Where adaptation shifts us horizontally to a different context, optimization pushes us to a level of excellence within an existing context. It has everything to do with improvement within a current position.

In other words, optimization only happens within a context that already exists and oftentimes only accomplishes marginal change.

In the big picture of history, nobody is going to care whether we adapted or optimized! It's simply not very memorable (nor interesting).

On the other hand, EVERYONE will care about how we innovated. Innovators create other innovators. Have you ever learned how to lead a business from someone who knows nothing about business? Unlikely. The same is true here. When you learn how to innovate, others will innovate with you. If adaptation is the only trick we have up our sleeve, then innovation is dead as we know it.

So, innovation is proactive. It's an entirely different beast. It doesn't just happen. It requires making a change regardless of circumstances. It involves making something happen to create the change. It is the pinnacle of courage and true leadership. Innovation happens when we put everything at risk for what has never been done before—something new!

To acquire the type of vision that causes true innovation, we need to fly high—high enough to see the things that are not yet done so that we can make them happen in our generation.

Innovation happens at the edge of chaos!

Let's brave that edge of chaos in our time and manifest something new that the history books will look back on as remarkable.

Innovation is our only option!

TO ACQUIRE THE TYPE OF VISION THAT CAUSES TRUE INNOVATION, WE NEED TO FLY HIGH—HIGH ENOUGH TO SEE THE THINGS THAT ARE NOT YET DONE SO THAT WE CAN MAKE THEM HAPPEN IN OUR GENERATION.

THIRTEEN

THE POWER OF THE OPEN DOOR

IT'S

ONE THING to know that God is calling you for a specific purpose. It's another thing to actually live that life of purpose.

Being called is simply not enough to live the life you were born to live.

When John had a vision on the island of Patmos, he saw a door open into heaven. As he looked at this door he heard a voice saying: "Come up here, and I will show you things which must take place after this" (Revelation 4:1, NKJV).

John's vantage point before he "came up" allowed him to "hear the call" of God, but he couldn't "see" the future that was behind the open door.

In order to gain access to the future that God has in store for us, we have to be able to leave our current position and paradigms and be elevated to a place where we gain three crucial things that "the open door" provides us with.

1) Perspective

This is the context in which your vision lives. We need to understand the context in order to interpret our vision. Think of perspective as the "map."

2) Direction

Once we have clarity of vision and an understanding of our context, we can determine a strategy to get to where we're going. Think of it as our "route."

3) Vision

You have to have clarity of vision in order to know where you are going. Think of it as your "destination" on a map.

Life has a tendency to bring us things that try to keep us from "seeing" and, therefore, prevent us from accessing everything that God has for us. Our minds are programmed to think based on what we've been told by the (often religious) culture we grew up in.

Perspective, direction, and vision are difficult to acquire if you remain in the valley. You have to walk up the mountain if you want to discover how vast the landscape of your life really is. Doing comes first; seeing comes second.

We have to break free from the indoctrination that imprisons our minds and keeps us "down there."

And that brings me to two pieces of very good news.

First, God factored in our imperfections (and, if we're being honest, sometimes, our stupidity) when He created His plan for our lives. You don't have to wring your hands over where the leap of faith will take you. God uses our good decisions and bad decisions to prosper us. So, if it's worst-case-scenario thinking that is holding you back from moving forward, you can officially put that to rest.

Second, when you move, God will open doors. There is a wide open door in heaven, and God is giving you permission to leave the old behind.

He's encouraging you to "come up here" and see!

Does He have your "yes"?

PERPETUAL REVOLUTION

STOP AND TAKE a look around. Have you noticed that life has a tendency to move forward whether we want it to or not? Let's go a level deeper—have you noticed that when life is stable and static for a period of time, we want things to move forward?

That's because human nature is to go against the grain of what is and what will be.

When the world is doing something new, God does something new. When God does something new, we must do something new.

What got us to where we are can't get us to where we're going!

As leaders, this is something important to understand. Why? Because every generation is supposed to contribute to the process God has in mind to further His kingdom across the earth. His kingdom is ever-increasing. Therefore, tomorrow will look different than today.

In other words, every generation is destined to disrupt the status quo that was created by those who went before them.

We are part of what I call a "Perpetual Revolution." A movement that is driven by an ever-advancing kingdom.

As leaders, we should be aware of this revolution so we can lead with progress and the future in mind.

When we understand that tomorrow will look different than today, we will lead with a less rigid mindset, allowing us to be flexible and agile enough to embrace the change the future demands.

The perpetual revolution is both a micro and macro-level phenomenon.

It will vie for your attention, calling you to participate in its grander vision for your life.

But the revolution is so much greater than its leading in your own life. The revolution demands generational change. We have to participate in the revolution through the lens of generational impact.

This means thinking about how what you do now with where the revolution is taking you will impact others.

Using our succession strategy as an example, the way we pass the baton to our successor will not only determine the quality with which that successor leads, but it will also determine how future generations of successors will lead.

Simply stated, as leaders, it's important to resist predefining the future based on what we've learned in our lifetime but rather keep an open mind as it relates to how the next generation will lead.

So, if we cling to our customs and resist the perpetual revolution, who is it impacting?

Our goal can't simply be to perpetuate what we've spent our lives building by demanding the same exact thing from those we raised.

What the future needs is not what we were able to provide others in the present.

That's our marching order—to create space for the revolution to thrive!

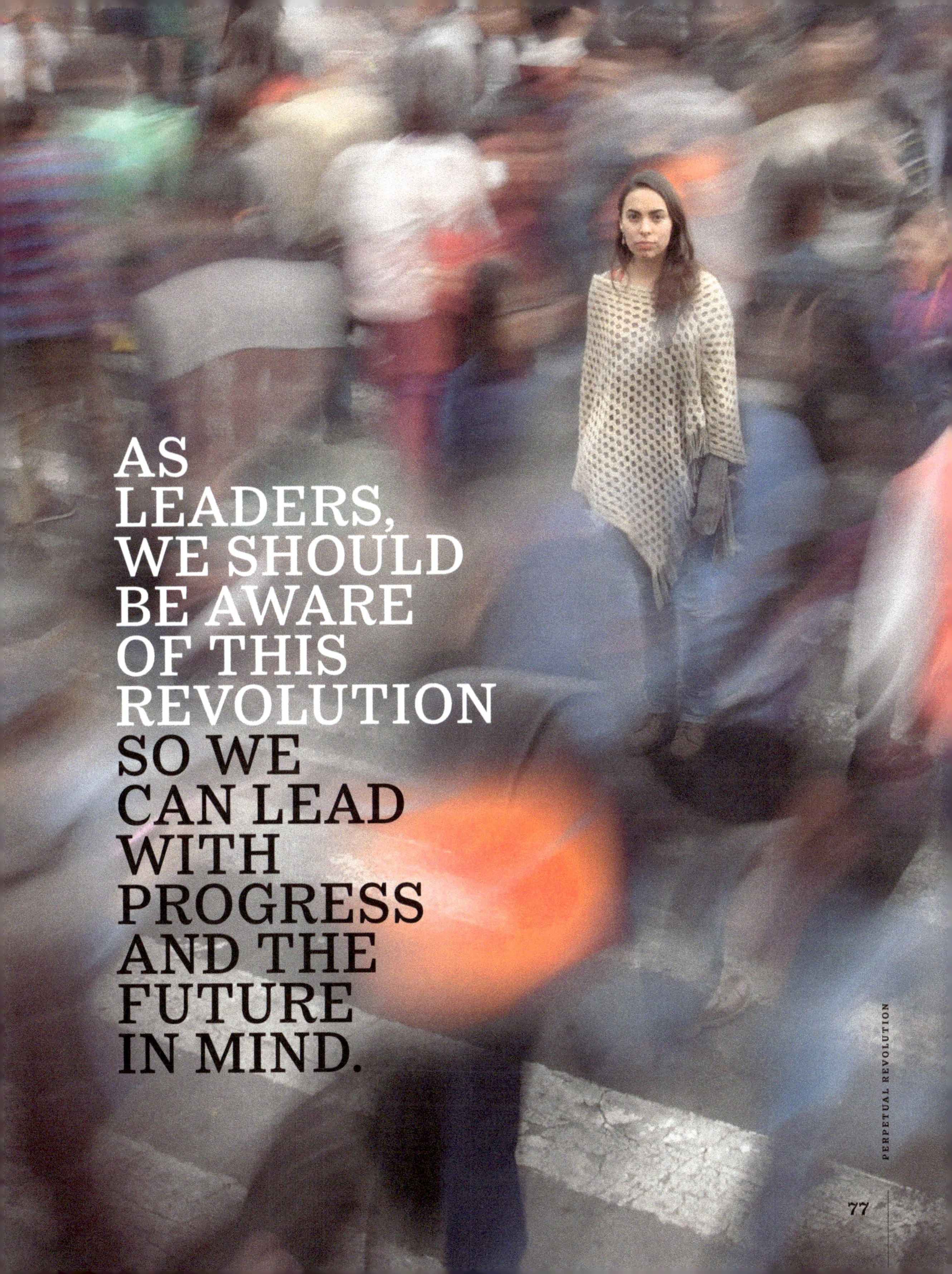

AS
LEADERS,
WE SHOULD
BE AWARE
OF THIS
REVOLUTION
SO WE
CAN LEAD
WITH
PROGRESS
AND THE
FUTURE
IN MIND.

15

THE ROOT OF ALL KINDS OF EVIL

MANY

SAY THAT MONEY is the root of all kinds of evil (or love of money). But by the same token, so is "the lack of money."

Poverty has the ability to make people do things that, under normal circumstances, they would never do.

One of the biggest tragedies in life happens when poverty causes someone to settle for something that is second (or third, or worse) best.

Whenever we experience lack, the temptation arises to trade our life for something that could potentially compensate for the deficit we're dealing with.

Suddenly, we settle for jobs we hate. Before long, we spend our days doing things we don't want to do simply because it helps us bridge the gap between what we have and what we need in order to survive. "I don't have enough" is a gateway to "this is my only option." It stifles imagination, creativity, ingenuity, and courage because we are too busy playing it safe. What it comes down to is this: we become more motivated to avoid risk than to run after reward.

And that's where the tragedy that I mentioned earlier begins to flourish—anything that you focus on will become bigger. If you focus on lack, you will find more lack in your life. It takes root . . . and becomes the root of all kinds of evil!

Welcome to the rat race!

There are only a few things more painful than to watch a man give up on his life's dreams and waste his life on doing things he despises, simply to make ends meet—even worse, a man who will not dare to dream in the first place!

Thankfully, God Himself declares in Isaiah 61:1 that He has good news for the poor.

God wants you to:
• Live a life you love.
• Live a life of significance.
• Live a life that adds value to others.
• Live a life that impacts the world around you.

This is not wishful thinking. In fact, it's God's heart that helps us break free from poverty and unleash us into a life of abundance, not just so that we can be blessed but also so that we can be a blessing to others. The kicker is we will never feel more blessed than when we are a blessing to others.

So, in a sense, we have a duty as God's chosen people to pursue, receive, and sow abundance.

God doesn't discourage wealth. Remember that money is God's, and it's one of His many gifts to humanity.

Let's not reject it. Let's take hold of it and share it with the world!

LET'S NOT REJECT IT. LET'S TAKE HOLD OF IT AND SHARE IT WITH THE WORLD!

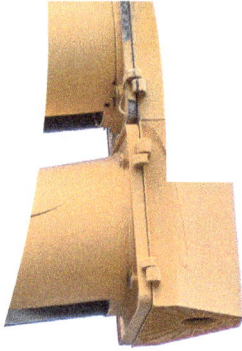

THE ANATOMY OF CHANGE

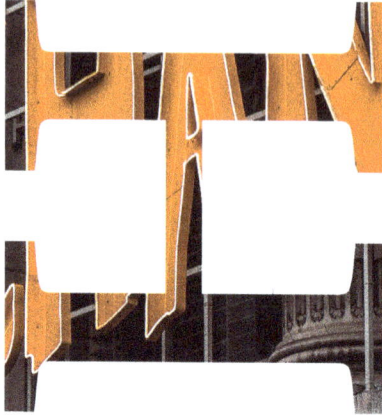

HOW MUCH do you love change? If I told you that your business operations or the systems you have in place weren't working, would you jump up and down for joy? If you had to start from scratch on everything you had built or, at best, redirect your focus and change course, would you wake up in the morning ecstatic that today, you get to reimagine what you already spent considerable time engineering in the first place?

I'm going to take a wild guess and assume that your answer to these questions was—absolutely not!

Congratulations! Welcome to the worldwide family of "I hate change!"

Unfortunately, we just don't have the luxury of evading change or delaying change. When it comes, it comes whether we like it or not!

When we begin to steer our rudders toward the shifting winds of change, we are setting ourselves up for progress and growth. When we get comfortable in life, it may cause us to fear or resist change, thus keeping us from growing.

So, we may not like change, but do we like stagnancy?

In order to experience continual growth, it's helpful to understand "the anatomy of the change."

Let's break down the process:

1) Acknowledge the need for change.

Come to terms with the fact that change is needed in order to grow.

2) Embrace change.

Now that you've come to terms that change is inevitable, be all in, and embrace it with everything you've got.

3) Anticipate change.

Continual growth will demand continual change. Just because something changed once, doesn't mean it isn't required again. Develop the expectation of imminent change.

4) Come to peace with the consequences of change.

Change comes with the reality of entering something new. You cannot enter something new unless you lose something old. Experiencing something "great" may require losing something "good."

5) Become a change agent.

Understanding and adopting the process will position you to become an agent of change yourself. You can cause change, and therefore growth, for others.

If you were to ask me what the most fundamental key to success is, the answer would be easy—change. Change may be scary, but you know what's scarier?

Looking back and realizing that you are exactly where you always were.

I promise you—if you begin to endear yourself to change and even fall in love with it, you'll be unstoppable.

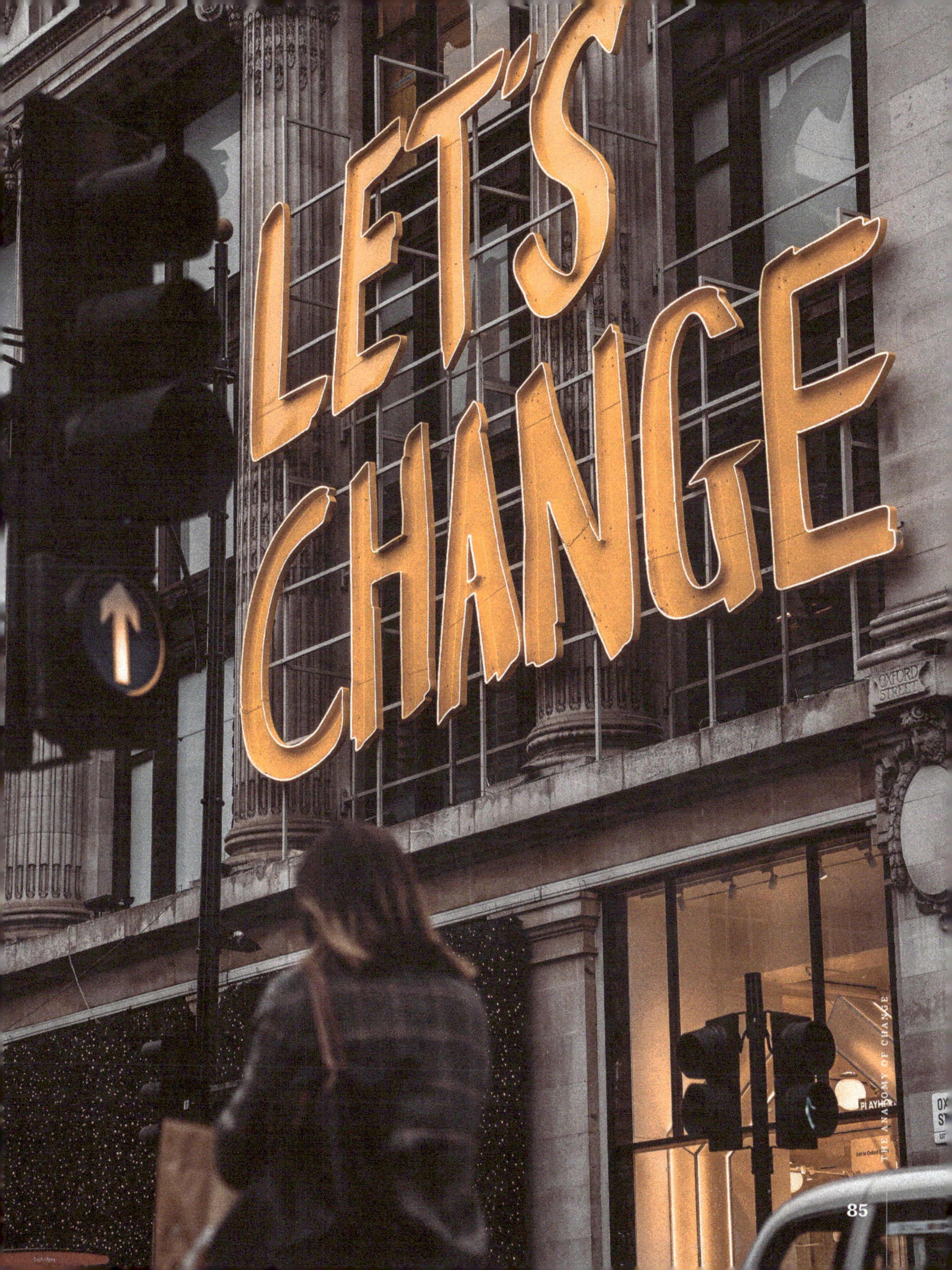
LET'S
CHANGE
OXFORD STREET

SEVENTEEN

OPPORTUNITY WITHOUT RESTRICTION

YOU'VE PROBABLY heard someone say before that "freedom" isn't "free," but it comes at a price.

Freedom is worth paying for, no matter how high the price tag.

That begs the question . . . how expensive is it?

Well, let's start here—freedom isn't automatic. It has to be defended. Before you know it, freedom can slip away from us, and we find ourselves imprisoned. Maybe we're not locked up in a jail cell, but mentally, socially, economically, and even spiritually, it's fairly easy for us to spiral into a place of confinement and lose the freedoms we once had.

Put another way, freedom is really just an idea if we don't work for it. Let's look at some practical examples of this.

You may be a Christian, but if you aren't living the way Jesus lived, are you really experiencing the fruits of Christianity? You may have access to foods that would support your health or even eradicate disease, but what good do they do if you don't incorporate them into your diet?

Availability isn't enough. You have to make the effort to maximize all that is available to you.

The same is true of freedom.

When we allow others to control the way we live our lives or when we allow a system to think on our behalf, we slowly transfer the responsibility that comes with freedom to those who exercise control.

The result of this process is a culture that is characterized by passivity and entitlement.

The Bible talks a lot about freedom. Freedom that offers us an opportunity without restriction.

God offers us access to a level of freedom that will shatter the chains of bondage that keep us small, insignificant, powerless, and without impact.

Study history and find that the countries that allowed freedom to govern their culture saw the most progress and innovation.

Yet, even as a believer, freedom isn't guaranteed. We can lose the freedom that God's kingdom offers us. As His church, we may have an "opportunity without restriction," but if we fail to take ownership and put that freedom to work, we don't really have it.

In fact, religion will restrict and suffocate the church by imposing often well-intended rules and regulations.

Just because our intentions are good doesn't guarantee a positive outcome of our efforts.

So, be assured that the fruit of true freedom—no matter how hard the fight—is indispensable.

Defend true freedom and live a life without restrictions!

DEFEND TRUE FREEDOM AND LIVE A LIFE WITHOUT RESTRIC- TIONS!

OPPORTUNITY WITHOUT RESTRICTION

COLOR OUTSIDE

THE LINES

THERE'S A PLACE for structure, boundaries, and parameters in our business, ministry, and even our families. They give you guardrails, they offer a sense of order when things feel a bit blurry, and, in some ways, they can even protect us.

But just like with anything else in life, you must be able to discern the difference between the protective qualities of a framework and the restrictive qualities of rules that keep you small.

You only need to look to children to understand the difference. You've likely seen a child in their own little world, crayons in hand, coloring their little hearts out. Before children develop fine motor skills, they cannot stay within the lines. The shape or figure had order—defined parametric lines—before they got their hands on it!

Yet, children are about the most innovative creatures in existence!

So, when I reference lines and colors, I'm talking about the defaults and templates that exist in our business and ministry worlds. There are certain procedures and patterns for how things are done. The catch is that, sometimes, these patterns actually hold us back from innovating.

When I was younger, I believed I was called into the ministry. I also believed, based on the ministry templates I'd been surrounded with my entire life, that this limited me to three branches of employment: a pastor, a missionary, or an itinerant speaker.

Today, I believe that God is far more creative than that!

When we go beyond our self-imposed limits, we'll find that there's so much more in store for us than the templates we've created for ourselves.

You have a unique gift—a unique color. Nobody else in all of history will possess the exact value and color that you bring to the table. Therefore, your color automatically falls outside the lines anybody else can draw for you.

There is only one you!

What does this mean? It means you're free to defy the expectations and limitations that culture or business models try to place on you.

This isn't an anti-authority message—it's an anti-conformity message.

So often, our greatest potential lies dormant because we subscribe to the notion that we need to mold ourselves into what's expected of us. When we kneel to expectations, we become a clone of others who kneel to those same expectations. You've got more in you.

Coloring outside the lines means that we embrace this truth:

No one structure can facilitate a world where every individual finds and maximizes his or her unique purpose.

This is my call to you today: get a little messy, break some culturally imposed rules, and color outside the lines!

NO ONE STRUCTURE CAN FACILITATE A WORLD WHERE EVERY INDIVIDUAL FINDS AND MAXIMIZES HIS OR HER UNIQUE PURPOSE.

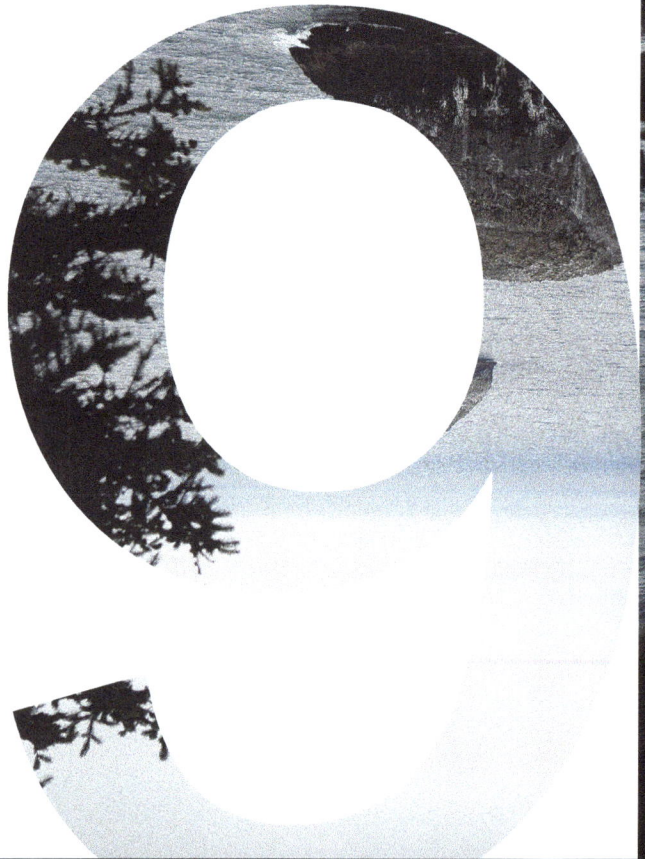

ARE YOU

A COPYCAT?

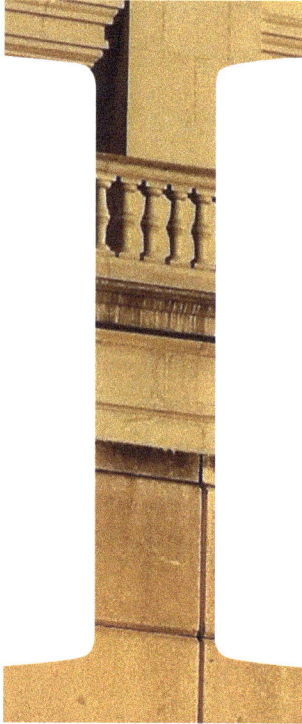

I KNOW, RIGHT? Strange question. Let me explain.

I love Ephesians 3:10 (NKJV): "To the intent that now the manifold wisdom of God might be made known by the church to the principalities and powers in the heavenly places."

God is not one-dimensional. He is "manifold." By divine design, He's created each individual to display and manifest an authentic aspect of who He is to the world. Our organizations should be unique, creative expressions of who He is, so the world around us can get to know Him.

Yet so many times, we are merely copycats of others: we choose the easy route by finding someone else who has a measure of success, and then we model our organization after them in an attempt to attain greatness. We look at big organizations and try to become like them.

I know it's tempting to copy ideas, models, and approaches based on established success stories. I'm sure you have heard the maxim, "Find success by doing what successful people do." While there's some truth and wisdom in this (leaders should always remain lifelong learners), we cross over into the danger zone when we become them. It's the fallacy of remaining relevant.

Instead of staying relevant by copying someone else's ideas, God wants us to create relevance—to set the standard. He wants us to become an expression of His divine inspiration, which, by definition, is unique and one-of-a-kind.

Ephesians 3:10 says that the principalities and powers need to be confronted by the infinitive spectrum of diverse creative expressions that display who He is. And He wants to do that through you and me!

Stop looking for "the next big thing" by modeling after others. Don't borrow from other people. Those things produce mediocrity at best because they were never meant for you in the first place.

Think about the men and women of the Bible whom God chose to free nations, reconcile them to Himself, and invite all of humankind to share in the glory of His Son. But, their victories were found in the unique giftings God gave them. Moses was chosen to lead the Israelites out of slavery and into the Promised Land. David was chosen because of his lifelong vocation as a shepherd and warrior—the perfect choice for a king (and a forerunner to Jesus). Paul was charged to be the apostle sent by Jesus Christ.

I think you get the picture. We are the body of Christ. This means that our callings are different—they are meant to complement each other—a feat that would be impossible if you were the same body part as someone else.

Today, seek inspiration for new and creative ideas—ones that will truly make a difference. You will be surprised at what you find on the other side.

Be someone who will make known yet another aspect of His manifold wisdom that has never been seen before!

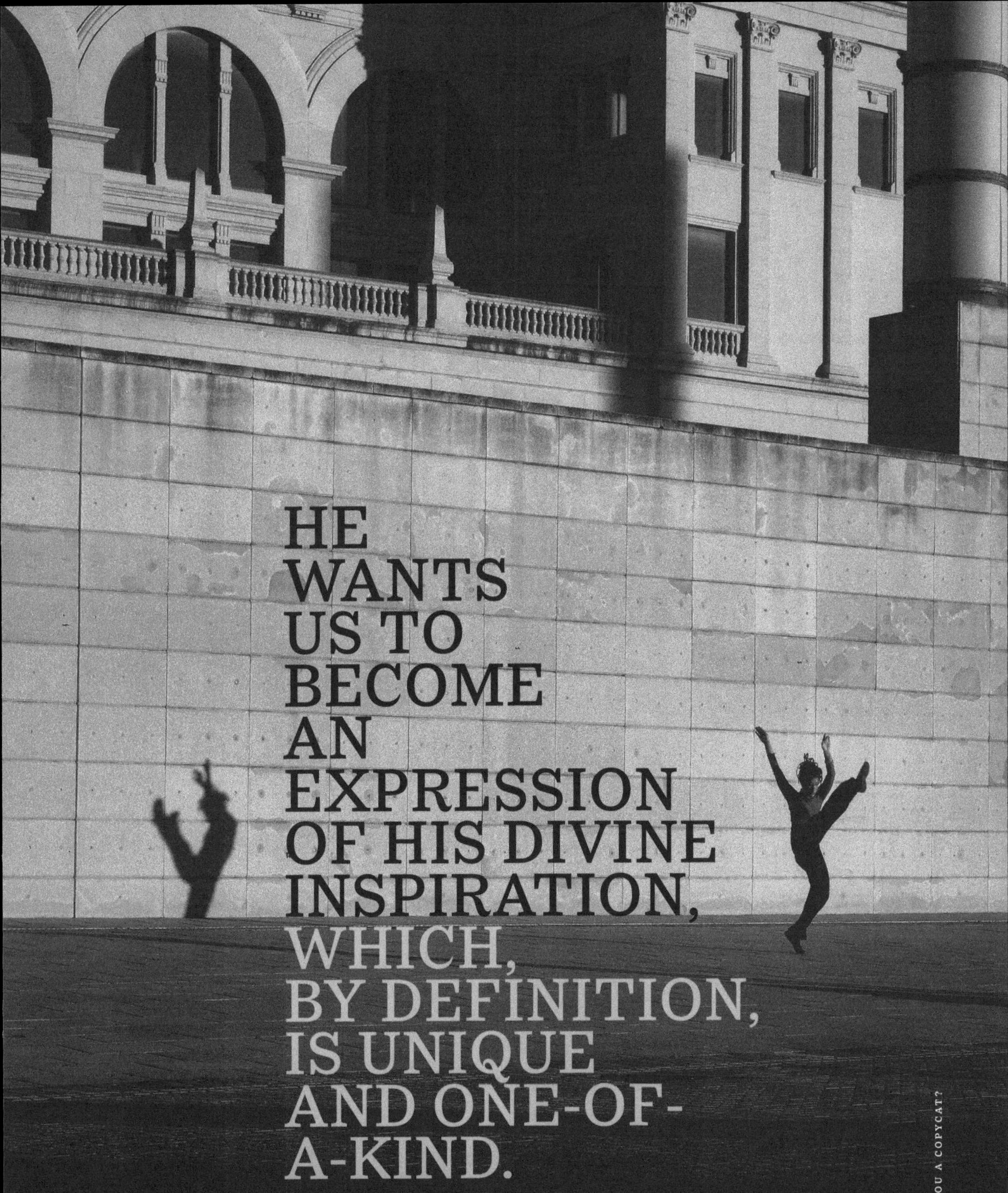

HE
WANTS
US TO
BECOME
AN
EXPRESSION
OF HIS DIVINE
INSPIRATION,
WHICH,
BY DEFINITION,
IS UNIQUE
AND ONE-OF-
A-KIND.

TODAY, SEEK INSPIRATION FOR NEW AND CREATIVE IDEAS— ONES THAT WILL TRULY MAKE A DIFFERENCE.

TWENTY

HOW TO
BUILD
THE
TALLEST
BUILDING
IN TOWN

W

WHEN YOU want to own the tallest building in the city, there are two strategies to accomplish that vision. The first is simply to tear down and demolish every building in town that is taller than yours. This is probably the easiest way to accomplish the desired outcome.

The second is to actually build the tallest building.

The problem with the first strategy is that tearing down everybody else doesn't actually make you any better. You are still you, exactly the same way you were before you tore the other person apart.

Sure, you may end up with the "tallest building in town," but only at the expense of others and not because your building ended up being any taller than before. You simply brought others down to your level of mediocrity.

It's a spirit of competition that leads us down this path. A spirit that shouldn't be part of our thinking to begin with. In fact, it may be worth asking the question of whether or not the desire to build the tallest building is actually rooted in the right mindset.

Could there be an alternative option that will allow you to be successful without having to "beat" someone else?

So often, we tend to focus on how we can earn more points on the scoreboard, not realizing the scoreboard we're looking at is referencing how we rank in a world of mediocrity. The best thing that can happen to us within that "paradigm" is that you and I become the best mediocre versions of ourselves that we can possibly become.

If that's the game you want to play, then you should certainly keep doing what you are doing. Who knows, maybe you can do a little better than that person next door.

There's another option—and in my opinion—a much better option. One that will not only enable you to build the skyscraper you are dreaming of building but will also allow you to recruit others who are doing better than you.

That's right—your "competition" can become your collaborators. If you've got other builders on your side, your building will grow much taller than you could have built on your own.

So, you start by refusing to operate in a world of mediocrity. You set yourself apart the way God already has.

Competition creates an illusion of success. Let's be honest. Business owners hustling and measuring themselves against other successful business owners put off an air of higher-level competency, and ambitious leaders are drawn to that.

But you have to be really careful. You have to see through that because the moment you are lured in by the spirit of competition is the moment you put yourself at risk of eating from their table instead of the table that God has prepared for you.

Make no mistake—you are a one-of-a-kind builder. The value you bring knows no competition.

IF YOU'VE GOT OTHER BUILDERS ON YOUR SIDE, YOUR BUILDING WILL GROW MUCH TALLER THAN YOU COULD HAVE BUILT ON YOUR OWN.

BUSINESS OWNERS HUSTLING AND MEASURING THEMSELVES AGAINST OTHER SUCCESSFUL BUSINESS OWNERS PUT OFF AN AIR OF HIGHER-LEVEL COMPETENCY, AND AMBITIOUS LEADERS ARE DRAWN TO THAT.

TWENTY ONE

OPPORTUNITY VS.

RESPONSIBILITY

OPPORTUNITY VS. RESPONSIBILITY

If

I WERE Moses at the burning bush, I can imagine that my ego would have been stroked.

Think about it. The word of the Lord came to him through a supernatural encounter with God Himself.

That must have been quite the experience and quite the ego boost! Think about a time when you were hand-selected to do something that you felt completely unequipped for. Pretty flattering, right? Obviously, someone saw something in you that you didn't see. Someone observed you, evaluated you, and made a judgment call about you—"Yep, that's the one!"

But what happened after you were presented with the opportunity? What did you do with it?

Moses received his mandate with great humility, and because of that, he did something beyond the opportunity that was laid before him. He stewarded the responsibility attached to the opportunity.

Moses was mandated to do some pretty remarkable things. In that moment at the burning bush, God promised to give him a platform and a ministry that he had never had before.

Moses was destined to speak to the masses (and remember, this was without the internet). The whole nation was about to get to know him.

Can you imagine this level of responsibility? All eyes on you, with the guarantee of criticism, slander, and endless accusations.

BUT . . .

This responsibility also came with the guarantee of supernatural deliverance, empowerment, and redemption. How rewarding would that be!

Not only did Moses have a supernatural experience and a profound encounter with the word of the Lord, but he was also given the ability to demonstrate some pretty powerful signs as he was sent to confront one of the most powerful strongholds in human history.

It was quite an amazing opportunity.

But here's the deal. When God is giving you a message, it's not enough to admire and marvel at the opportunity. That's part of the package, yes. That's where it begins. But that message comes with responsibility. Though responsibility can often seem burdensome—the honor is much greater. God Himself chose you to carry out a duty that will change the world.

You see, something happens when you ask God to use you. When God answers your prayer, don't shrink back from the responsibility that comes with the opportunity. There's no joy in opportunity without action.

As someone once said, "With great power comes great responsibility."

In fact, your responsibility IS the opportunity!

AS SOMEONE ONCE SAID, "WITH GREAT POWER COMES GREAT RESPON-SIBILITY." IN FACT, YOUR RESPON-SIBILITY IS THE OPPOR-TUNITY!

YOU HAVE BEEN ROBBED!

IN THE BOOK

OF JOHN, we find the following scripture:

"The thief comes only to steal and kill and destroy; I have come that they may have life, and have it to the full" (John 10:10, NIV).

In other words, you (and I) will face opposition. There is a force out there that wants to keep us from experiencing the fullness of God working in and through our lives.

Many times, "the thief " manifests himself in very obvious ways. He shows his true nature by attempting to bring destruction, sickness, poverty, and death in order to keep us from greatness.

However, could it be that the thief comes to steal from us in a far more subtle manner?

Could it be that the most effective way the thief steals from us is by making us believe that the comfortable life we live is, in fact, the abundance that God has for us?

That's blind robbery at its finest!

This shouldn't be all that surprising. The Bible refers to the serpent as craftier than any other creature God has created. Crafty. Not conspicuous.

He gives it everything he's got to keep us sleepy and unaware; all the while, God has so much more for us to experience!

What if the thief comes to make us believe that life, as it is, is as good as it gets?

God has more for you than the life you live today. There is an abundance outside of your current paradigm that He wants you to tap into.

Now, some of you might be content with where you are in life.

You have your job, your home, your car, your dog, your ministry, and your family, and life is pretty great.

Really, what more do you need? I get it!

Don't rock the boat. If you are fulfilled, I'm not advocating that you disturb that.

BUT, if this is you, then what I'm about to share is very important for you to understand.

Are you ready?

Here it is: it's not all about you!

Don't be blessed for yourself (though that's great)! Be blessed to be a blessing to those around you.

You have surely needed those blessings at some point in your life. Others will need them too!

DON'T
BE
BLESSED
FOR
YOURSELF
(THOUGH
THAT'S
GREAT)!
**BE BLESSED
TO BE
A BLESSING
TO THOSE
AROUND YOU.**

PROGRESSIVE REVELATION

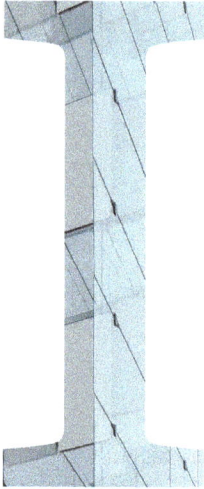

INFORMATION WITHOUT context is useless!

Let's say someone makes the statement, "It's freezing cold!" This statement by itself doesn't tell me anything as it relates to what needs to be believed about the situation. The context in which it is spoken will determine whether "freezing cold" is a good or a bad thing.

If it's freezing cold inside my kitchen freezer, I'm happy. But if it's freezing cold in my living room, I would definitely prefer for it to be warmer.

So "context" is required before putting information to use.

Information is only as valuable as the context in which it exists.

Revelation is information given to us by God Himself. Yet, revelation needs context for it to be useful to us.

The lack of contextual understanding will force a limitation on revelation. In fact, it could potentially make it useless or, worse, counterproductive to God's objectives.

Over time, God may try to "widen our lens" so that we can gain additional insight into something that He has already revealed to us.

I call this dynamic "progressive revelation."

So let's keep an open mind!

Let me give you a practical example. When it comes to finances, we often quote from the book of Malachi 3.

We can't rob God; we have to give!

Our tithes and offerings are crucial in opening up the windows of heaven. Besides, we don't want to invite the devourer into our lives to keep us from being blessed by God.

So we simply give, just to keep the windows open. Nothing wrong with that.

But then the revelation progresses. Yes, you definitely want to continue to give, but you start to understand that unless we come to the place of "death" in our giving, the seed will not bear fruit. In John 12:24 (NKJV), Jesus puts it this way:

"Most assuredly, I say to you, unless a grain of wheat falls into the ground and dies, it remains alone; but if it dies, it produces much grain."

We suddenly start to look at the same thing differently. Now you're starting to see that it's better to give than to receive, regardless of the return I may or may not get.

But what if it doesn't stop there? What if there is yet another way to look at the same thing?

Instead of waiting for the windows of heaven to open, you start to understand that, in fact, YOU are a window that God can choose to open and close to pour out blessings to others.

You understand that wherever we are and wherever we go, we become windows at God's disposal. He can choose at any given time to use us to be a window of blessing. He can open us up or close us at His discretion. Why? Because we are blessed to be a blessing to others.

Never settle when it comes to revelation.

There is always something more to understand. There is always a higher way of thinking and a broader perspective to discover.

INSTEAD OF WAITING FOR THE WINDOWS OF HEAVEN TO OPEN, YOU START TO UNDERSTAND THAT, IN FACT, YOU ARE A WINDOW THAT GOD CAN CHOOSE TO OPEN AND CLOSE TO POUR OUT BLESSINGS TO OTHERS.

THERE IS ALWAYS SOMETHING MORE TO UNDERSTAND. THERE IS ALWAYS A HIGHER WAY OF THINKING AND A BROADER PERSPECTIVE TO DISCOVER.

TWENTY FOUR

ALL YOU NEED VS. ALL YOU CAN GET

OFTENTIMES,

I HEAR people say that "the Bible is all you need in your life." While perhaps that may be a true statement, let me ask you a question.

Would you prefer to get what you need, or would you rather receive what Paul defines as "exceedingly abundantly above all that we ask or think" (Ephesians 3:20, NKJV)?

Sure, the Bible will provide you with everything needed in order to make it to the finish line (and, to be fair, probably much more). However, just having your basic needs met is no fun. Believe me, I've been there (I'm sure you have too).

God is so much bigger than the Bible!

Before you judge this statement, please hear me out. It's actually very simple, and the truth is, I didn't come up with this statement myself.

Scripture itself teaches us that what's written in the Bible is just a very tiny fraction of so much more that exists in God's kingdom. So much more that could be available to us if we can think beyond "just" the Scriptures.

God has done and will do exceedingly abundantly more than what's in the Bible.

Who decided that the book of Acts had to stop after twenty-eight chapters? Somewhere along the way, someone made that call. But do we really believe that all of Acts is just twenty-eight chapters worth of content?

In the New Testament, John explains that there is so much more about Jesus than what is written in the Bible. In fact, he states that if we were to document the full manifestation of Him, "The world itself could not contain the books that would be written" (Acts 21:25, ESV).

Think about that for a moment.

Imagine if we had all of those books. Those books that would be written if the world itself could contain them. The question is . . . could you?!

Sometimes, it's hard enough to devote ourselves to reading the Bible. Here's my point: just because God packaged His word in a book doesn't mean His work is bound by pages.

Could it be that the splendor of God's glory is displayed most brightly when He blows our minds? When He accomplishes something we didn't even know was in the realm of possibility—because our noses are only in one book?

Now, THAT sounds like our God.

COULD IT BE THAT THE SPLENDOR OF GOD'S GLORY IS DISPLAYED MOST BRIGHTLY WHEN HE BLOWS OUR MINDS?

TWENTY FIVE

UNIFORMITY VS. DIVERSITY

AS (CHURCH) LEADERS, we often feel responsible for providing vision for the people we serve.

You see, when people lack vision, it's sometimes easier to provide it for them than to facilitate an environment for them to get their own.

I know this first hand because I've tried both!

While God may have a "collective vision" for mankind on a macro level, He also desired to impart individual vision to each person on a micro level. The sum of the individual dreams and visions of all people will ultimately fulfill God's macro vision for creation.

Why is this so important to understand, you ask?

Well, when we as leaders provide a vision for a group of people, we could potentially keep them from discovering and fulfilling their own.

There comes a time when every person will grow up and "leave his father and mother" to form his own family and create the future he envisions for himself (Genesis 2:24). Sure, there is a time and place for children to be part of the vision of the parent and serve in the house they grow up in. However, there comes a moment when something healthy turns toxic as the child reaches a level of maturity.

Deep down inside of you is the desire for what I call "righteous independence" that is put there by God Himself when He created you.

The danger of collective vision of any kind of organization, institution, or church is that the more committed you are to that collective vision, the more you start to look like everyone else who is committed to that vision.

While on the surface, this type of uniformity seems noble, on a deeper level, it contradicts the culture of diversity that God has in mind for His people.

Perhaps there's a balance to strike. But every good thing can become a not-so-good thing (or even an excessive thing). Exercise is good, but too much of it can become excessive. Sleep is great for you, but too much sleep is associated with a lot of serious health issues.

In the same way, too much collective vision is a slippery slope. Value it in its right season. Take it in the proper doses.

So if you feel suffocated by the environment you're in on a creative, visionary level, it may be a sign of maturity. It may be time to leave and create something of your own.

Value diversity over uniformity!

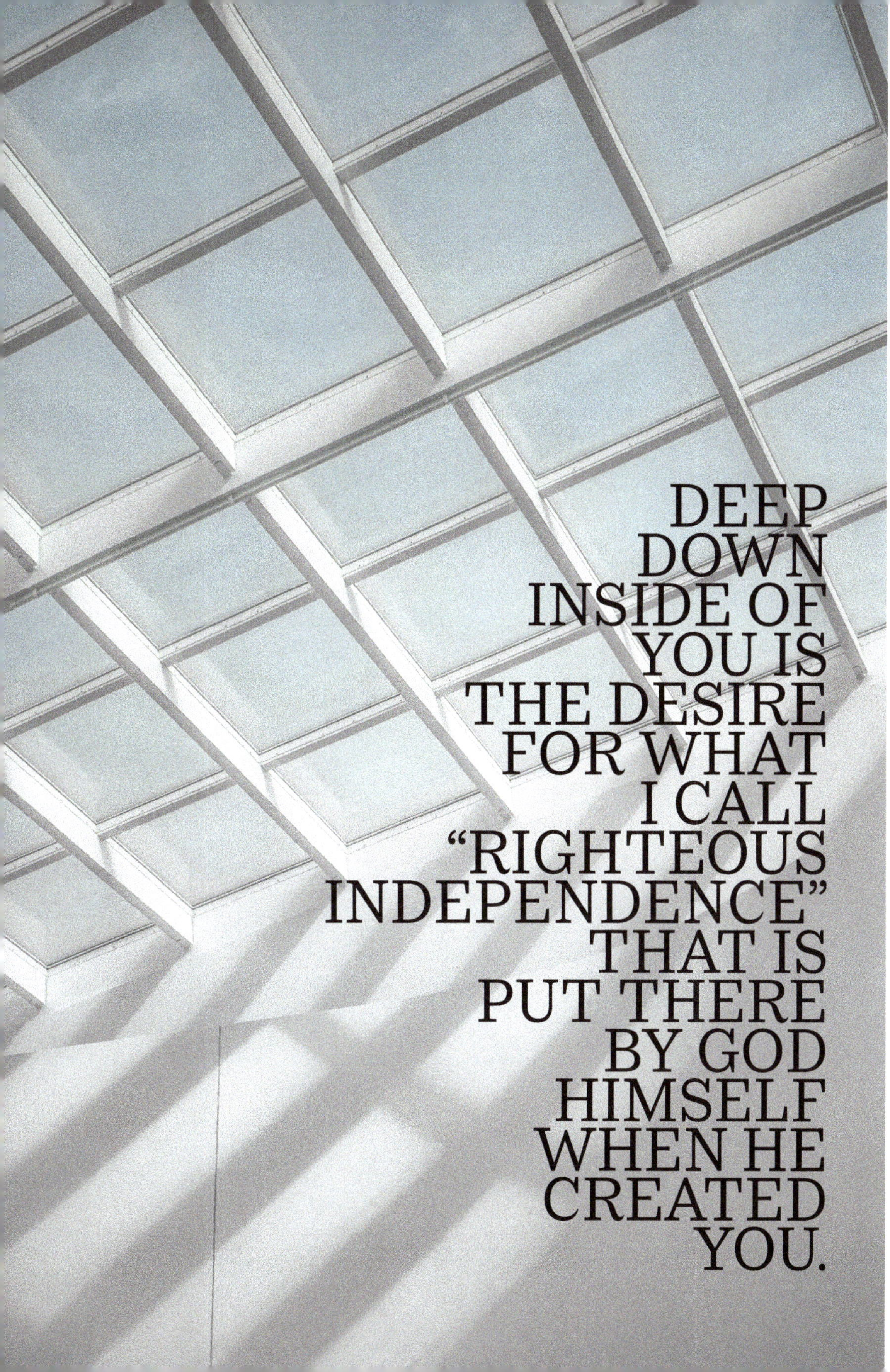

DEEP
DOWN
INSIDE OF
YOU IS
THE DESIRE
FOR WHAT
I CALL
"RIGHTEOUS
INDEPENDENCE"
THAT IS
PUT THERE
BY GOD
HIMSELF
WHEN HE
CREATED
YOU.

TWENTY SIX

THEOLOGY VS. EXPERIENCE

COULD IT BE that God is less interested in our theology than He is in our experience?

The longer I live, the more I'm convinced this is the case. At least, I like to believe so.

You see, if "accurate theology" was most important to God, we would all be in trouble by now. The truth is that nobody has figured it all out. We're all wrong somewhere.

It really doesn't matter how much of a "Bible-believing Christian" you are; everybody's interpretation of that Bible lacks accuracy on some level.

The real truth is that Jesus (or Paul, for that matter) didn't even have a Bible, nor did He go to church, by the way.

Paul says it this way:

"For the kingdom of God is not in word, but in power" (1 Corinthians 4:20, NKJV).

In other words, "power" trumps "word" (or "experience" trumps "theology").

I know this may be controversial for some of us, but honestly, this is good news for all of us. It means that we can experience His kingdom, even when we are theologically wrong.

What a liberating thought!

There's more.

While we could talk all day long about the possible reasons why biblical theology has undergone a kind of turbo-speed mitosis (that's quite a rabbit hole), perhaps there's something valuable to that.

We tend to view varying theological perspectives as dividing, grating, and maybe even ignorant. Maybe it's time to flip that script.

Here's why.

God allows error so long as we acknowledge our natural-born proclivity to err and continue to seek Him for the answers. As we wait for answers, we have the opportunity to learn from others, get curious about their theological takes, and, as a result, navigate the beautiful complexities of relationships.

Are you getting what I'm describing? Experience!

See, God wired our brains to think differently. At some point, we will all be wrong, and we will all be right. That was always God's Plan A.

While I'm not encouraging you to stop educating yourself, let yourself off the hook—you don't have to have it all figured out. You don't have to get your theology perfect before you can experience the power of His kingdom.

Because chances are that I (and probably you) will never experience anything otherwise.

So, let's not take ourselves too seriously when it comes to our theology.

No matter which way you slice it— we're all wrong!

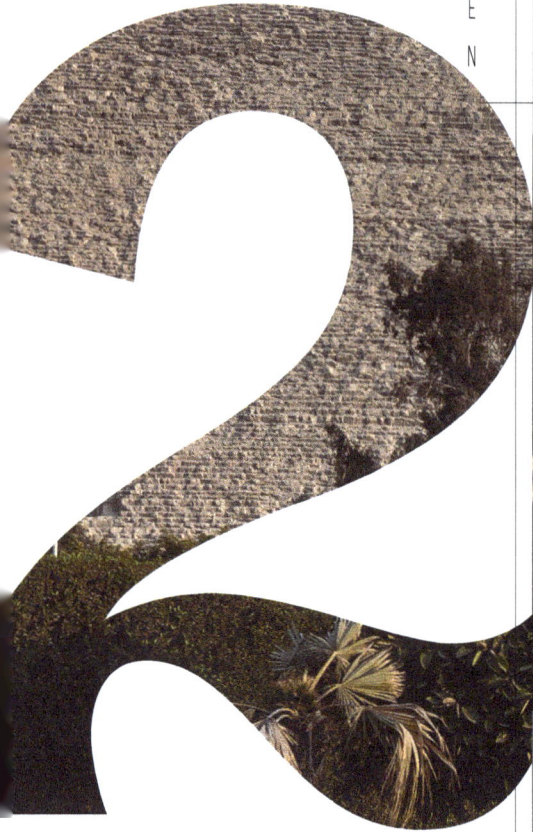
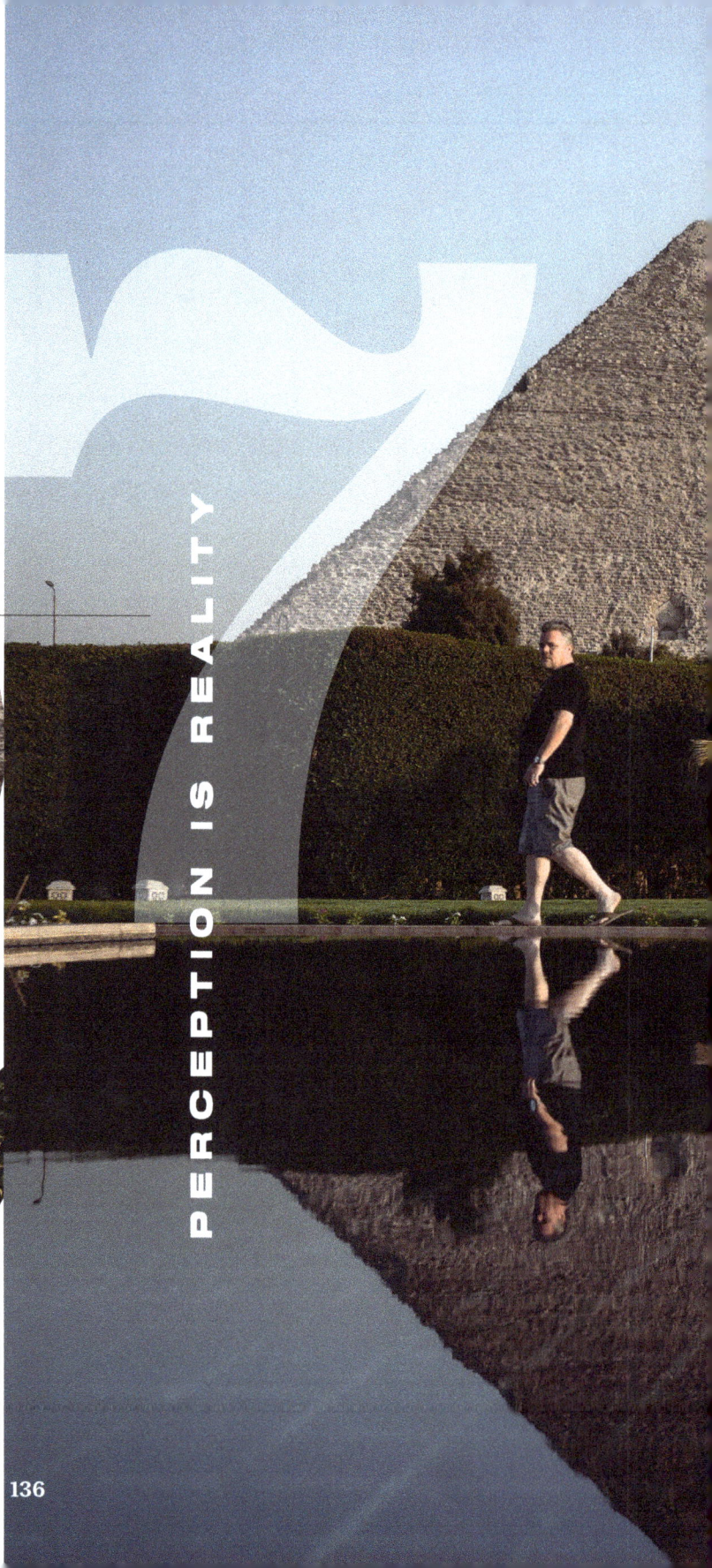

2 7

PERCEPTION IS REALITY

The

OTHER DAY, I was reading in the book of Numbers where it says: "So they said to one another, 'Let us select a leader and return to Egypt'" (14:4, NKJV).

Wow! Really?

Although this may not sound like a ground-breaking, earth-shaking verse, it's actually pretty profound.

Here are God's people, just having escaped the horrible regime of Pharaoh in the land of Egypt, where they had been stuck for hundreds of years. They are about to step into the promise that they had heard about from their ancestors for centuries. As they found themselves at a pivotal point in history and were going to actually inherit that promise, their conclusion was that they really needed to "select a leader and return to Egypt."

What was inside of them that was so powerful it would keep them from God's promise—the promise they were so close to inheriting? And what do we as leaders need to learn from their mistakes that will prevent us from falling into the same trap?

As I was meditating on these questions, I came to the conclusion that their perception of the truth was the thing that kept them from all that God had in store for them.

Somehow, they had come to believe that it was better to die in Egypt than it was to die in the Promised Land. Something in them made them default back to the situation that had mentally conditioned them for abuse for 430 years.

The paradigm that was formed over the course of their captivity caused them to make this statement:

And all the children of Israel complained against Moses and Aaron, and the whole congregation said to them, "If only we had died in the land of Egypt! Or if only we had died in this wilderness! Why has the Lord brought us to this land to fall by the sword, that our wives and children should become victims? Would it not be better for us to return to Egypt?" (Numbers 14:2-3, NKJV)

According to their own report, there were three possible outcomes of their situation:

1) Die in Egypt
2) Die in the wilderness
3) Die in the Promised Land

My conclusion: let's forget the fact that there was actually a fourth option which was to LIVE in the land of promise. According to their own perception, they were going to die in all three scenarios. Yet, for whatever reason, it seemed much better for them to die in captivity or in the wilderness than it was to die in a place of freedom and promise.

The ways in which we are conditioned will be the direction we run if we don't hold onto—no, white knuckle—the promises we have from God. Egypt conditioned them, and they didn't trust God, so they wanted to run back to their abusers. This is picture-perfect Stockholm Syndrome.

Their perceptions were illusions, yet reality—to them.

The big question is . . .

What makes us believe that we are any different?

TWENTY EIGHT

ENTER THE
INEVITABLE
CONFLICT

ENTER THE INEVITABLE CONFLICT

CONFLICT IS a funny thing. It's unavoidable. Pervasive yet specific. Awkward yet at the same time familiar.

Not to mention—confusing.

Conflict always creates chaos, chaos always creates uncertainty, and uncertainty always creates excitement (NOT the good kind!)—and likely, a great deal of resistance.

We don't have to look any further than the account of David and King Saul.

David returned home from leading Saul's army to victory over the Philistines. In 1 Samuel 18:7 (NKJV), we read that the women came out with their tambourines, singing, "Saul has slain his thousands, and David his ten thousands."

It was at this moment that something happened. Something that couldn't be reversed. Angered by the attention given to David, Saul "eyed David from that day forward" (v. 9). The women's song catalyzed a conflict. A war that would linger on for a long time, but David would inevitably win.

He was destined not to perpetuate the kingdom that had been built under Saul but to establish something that had never been done before. In fact, the vision that burned inside David's heart would ultimately erase all that Saul had built over the forty years that he ruled as king.

I believe that the church finds itself in a similar situation today. We are in a place we have never questioned before because it was something that had always been there. We grew up in it. It defined us. It was part of us. We were part of it.

And if you are a leader, you have likely been appointed to, just like King David, in some capacity, steer the church in the direction of the "new thing" God wants to do, which means . . .

We can't be a King Saul. We have to be a David.

King Saul was determined to keep his kingdom under his thumb instead of giving God the space to usher in change and mobility. Saul said, "I'm king. The kingdom will look like this, be like this, and stay like this because I'm in charge." In other words, King Saul ruled with the philosophy that he wouldn't change with God's movement; no, God's movement would have to change for him.

Unfortunately (or should I say, fortunately), the King Saul attitude will never work out in our favor. We can fight tooth and nail the changes going on in the church, but we aren't powerful enough to thwart God's plan for the future of the church.

Why make it hard on ourselves?

Hopefully, you have become uncomfortable with where we are. Unsatisfied. You can't quite put your finger on it, but it is there. A sense of unease that there must be something more. Something better. Something greater that God has in store for His people.

Something bigger and better for you and me.

Sounds like the David in you.

WE CAN FIGHT TOOTH AND NAIL THE CHANGES GOING ON IN THE CHURCH BUT WE AREN'T POWERFUL ENOUGH TO THWART GOD'S PLAN FOR THE FUTURE OF THE CHURCH

HOW ACCURATE IS THE STORY WE TELL?

HAVE YOU ever read the countless stories of men and women in the Bible and thought to yourself, "How could they be so stupid? So disloyal to God? So violent? So rebellious?"

Today is meant to be a bit confrontational (for myself included)!

After hundreds of years of suffering, God delivered several million people from slavery as Moses led them out of Egypt.

This powerful and supernatural experience undeniably changed the trajectory of a nation forever. God had not forgotten them. As He had heard the cry of the people, He decided to demonstrate His power and might and deliver His people from an "impossible" situation.

God had become so real to the people that His presence became undeniable.

Yet just a few days later, those same people took the little they owned and threw it into "Aaron's offering" so they could build a golden idol that would become a false representation of their deliverance.

For the most part, we no longer have golden idols or carved wooden images that we worship.

But we need to keep in mind something very important:

Just because our representations of God look different, they really aren't all that different. The changing cultural milieu doesn't exactly change the fact that oftentimes, we're doing the same thing.

That's the confrontational part.

We are no different than they are. In fact, we couldn't be more similar.

See, if we're being honest, it's quite counterintuitive for us to honor and place our faith in something that we cannot see. While He makes Himself known to us in countless ways (and often, in BIG ways), we cannot see God with our eyes, and humans like proof. They like physical evidence of the object of their comfort.

So, where there are gaps in the physical, we tend to fill them with our own stories, our own interpretations, and our own preferences that create false stories.

Why am I sharing this?

Apparently, it's possible to have a true, supernatural experience with God while creating something that completely misrepresents that experience to the outside world.

This makes me wonder . . .

What sacrifices have we made to build something that completely misrepresented God's undeniable presence in our lives?

Is the story we tell the world accurate? Or are we misrepresenting Him, as well?

If it happened to the Israelites, it can certainly happen to us.

Let's at least consider the possibility. Don't turn your breakthrough into the wrong story.

WHILE
HE MAKES
HIMSELF
KNOWN
TO US IN
COUNTLESS
WAYS (AND
OFTEN, IN
BIG WAYS),
WE CANNOT
SEE GOD
WITH OUR
EYES, AND
HUMANS
LIKE
PROOF.

HOW "KNOWLEDGE" OF GOOD WILL KILL YOU

We

FIND OURSELVES in a battle. Not a battle between "Good and Evil," as many people say, but a battle between "Life and Death."

Believe me, there is a big difference!

As people, we seem to be predisposed to fight the battle between "good and evil" or "right and wrong." We look at the world through a lens that pushes us to make a "judgment call" on whether something is "good" or "bad." Once we make up our mind about a situation, verbalizing our conclusion is seen as a virtue (or even perceived as "radical faith").

While this seems noble on the surface, when you dig a little deeper, you'll draw a different conclusion.

You see, when God created us, He placed us in an environment where there were two trees (Genesis 2:8-9):

1) The Tree of the Knowledge of Good and Evil

2) The Tree of Life

Then it reads:

"Of every tree of the garden you may freely eat; but of the tree of the knowledge of good and evil you shall not eat, for in the day that you eat of it you shall surely die" (Genesis 2:16-17, NKJV).

Unlike common belief, knowledge of good AND evil grows on the same tree. A tree that produces death.

One way to look at this is that knowledge of "what's right" will lead to death just as much as knowledge of "evil" does.

In other words, being right is irrelevant! In fact, it gets you killed.

The question is not whether something is "good" or "bad." The right question to ask is, "How do my actions bring life to the situation?"

Let's leave the real "judging" up to God, and let's stay in our own lane.

True radical faith comes from eating from the tree of life.

Forget about what's "good" (even when you know you're right) because knowledge of good will ultimately kill you!

What tree will you eat from?

155

TRUE
RADICAL
FAITH
COMES
FROM
EATING
FROM
THE
TREE
OF LIFE.

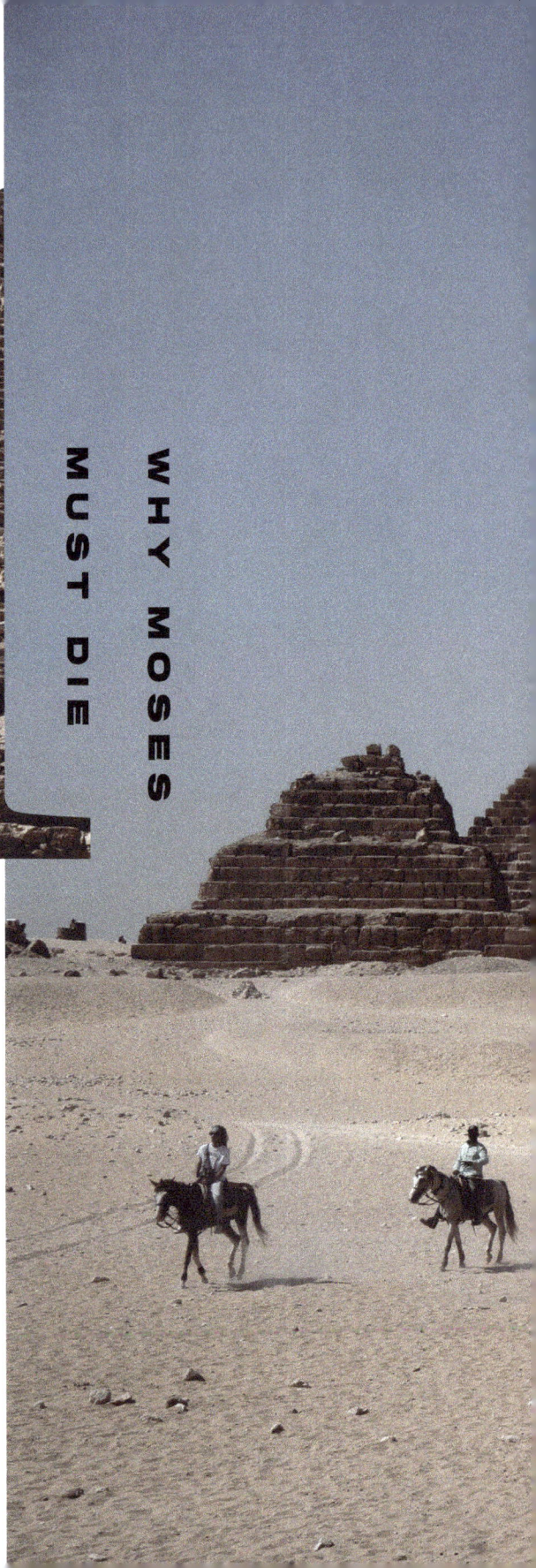

31

WHY MOSES MUST DIE

E

WAS MOSES who was able to lead God's people successfully for forty years in unfavorable circumstances.

Many of us would kill for a resume like that of Moses. He was a model leader everyone looked up to.

Yet Moses had to die in order for God's people to reach the next echelon of their journey and destiny. Not just physically but also mentally.

After spending forty years under Moses's leadership, Joshua had to accept both Moses's physical death as well as the death of the model of leadership he represented.

It had fulfilled its purpose. "Moses" had become obsolete for the season they were in. The "Moses way of thinking" had to be removed from Joshua's mind in order to enter the promises God had for him.

This new season required a whole new way of thinking and leading. Moses could no longer be used as a point of reference for what successful leadership looked like.

As seasons change, as assignments change, and as needs change, so must the positions of those people whom God used to accomplish older kingdom objectives. The good news is that this is never done to the detriment of His people. Every shift under the control of God is for the purpose of blessing ALL.

So, Moses's death really served God's higher purpose for change. This is especially important for leaders to understand because good leaders are forward-thinking. They, in many ways, determine the future of an organization or ministry. If they stay stuck in the past, so will everyone else who follows them.

Not to mention, an effective leader creates other leaders.

Leaders can't expect to train up new leaders if they won't let go of the old.

Keep this in mind.

The greater our knowledge of God's character and faithfulness, the more we WANT to serve His purposes and not our own. So even for Moses, perhaps we can assume he didn't take God's plan for his death too personally (or if he did, he remained yielded to God).

If we allow ourselves to step back and create some mental margin to hear what God has to say to us as leaders, we may hear those same words Joshua heard when God stated the obvious.

"Moses my servant is dead!" (Joshua 1:2, NIV)

Whether we like it or not, whatever got us to where we are can't get us to where we are going!

Sooner or later, we've got to align ourselves with the death of the old, even if the old got us to where we are today.

SOONER OR LATER, WE'VE GOT TO ALIGN OUR- SELVES WITH THE DEATH OF THE OLD, EVEN IF THE OLD GOT US TO WHERE WE ARE TODAY.

WHERE WE ARE CAN'T GET US

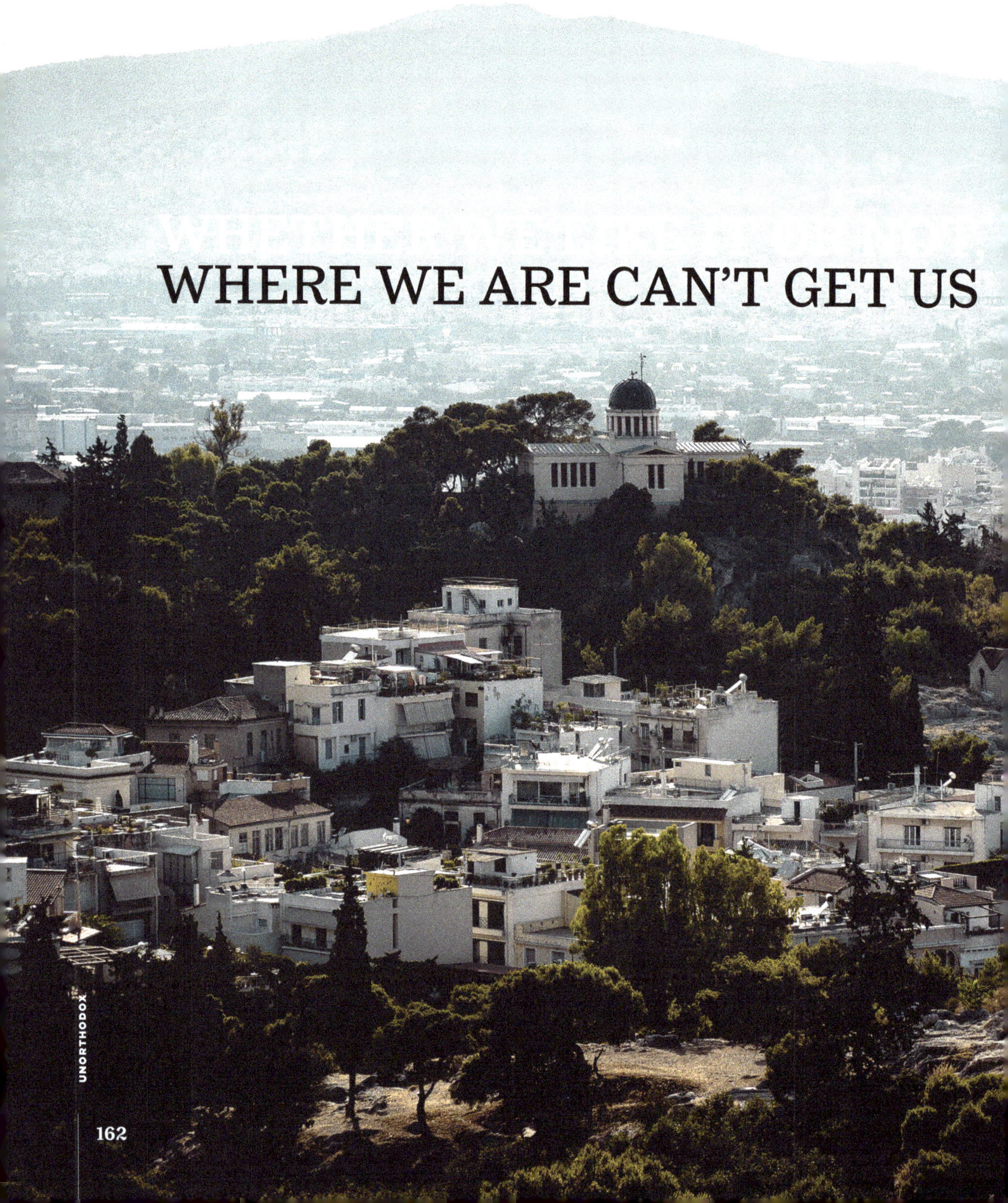

WHATEVER GOT US TO
TO WHERE WE ARE GOING!

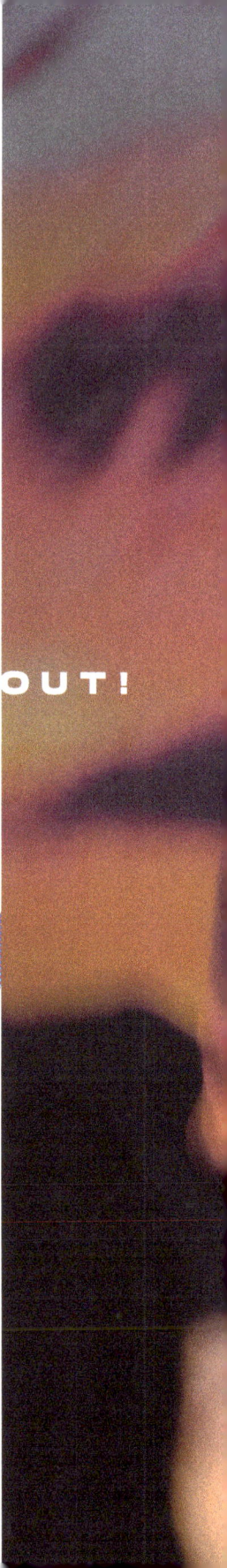

32

I'M FREAKING OUT!

REMEMBER THAT time when God's people were enslaved in Egypt for hundreds of years?

This story always freaked me out!

Why, you ask?

Well, the answer is simple. These Israelites were God's people. They were God's chosen ones. They were favored above all nations and had a covenant with God. They were not some random nation who ended up in a place they probably "deserved" to be in.

Apparently, it's possible to be in covenant and relationship with God and find yourself in a place where all your hard work, effort, and energy are spent to build something that is completely foreign to what God had in mind for his people.

You see, the efforts of God's people ultimately fortified the empire that had enslaved them for hundreds of years.

Wow! Could it be that this story is about us?

I think it is. We've all been in that confusing place where it seems like the path God paved for us is just . . .

not going as planned. Everywhere we look, there's a detour, pain, and obstacles.

Don't get me wrong. Barriers and hardship are not always indicative that we are veering off into the land of rebellion. In fact, many times, they could be green lights that are shouting, "Oh, this is hard?? You're doing something right! Keep going!"

But there's a difference between the opposition that faithful obedience brings and the opposition we create for ourselves. We have to cultivate discernment to tell the difference.

With that, here's the question of the day.

Is it possible that, like the people of Israel, our hard work, efforts, energy, and even money are contributing to the building of something that is contrary to what God had in mind that we should create?

Is it possible that we (God's people) are conditioned in our thinking (and therefore behavior) by hundreds of years of living life a certain way while all along our efforts have fortified "the enemy's position"?

If it happened to God's people back then, it can happen to us today. I would imagine it already has happened to you or may even be happening now.

We should at least consider the possibility that what we invest our lives in may not contribute to the advancement of the right thing.

So, what are you building?

167

THIRTY THREE

DEALING WITH DREAM HATERS

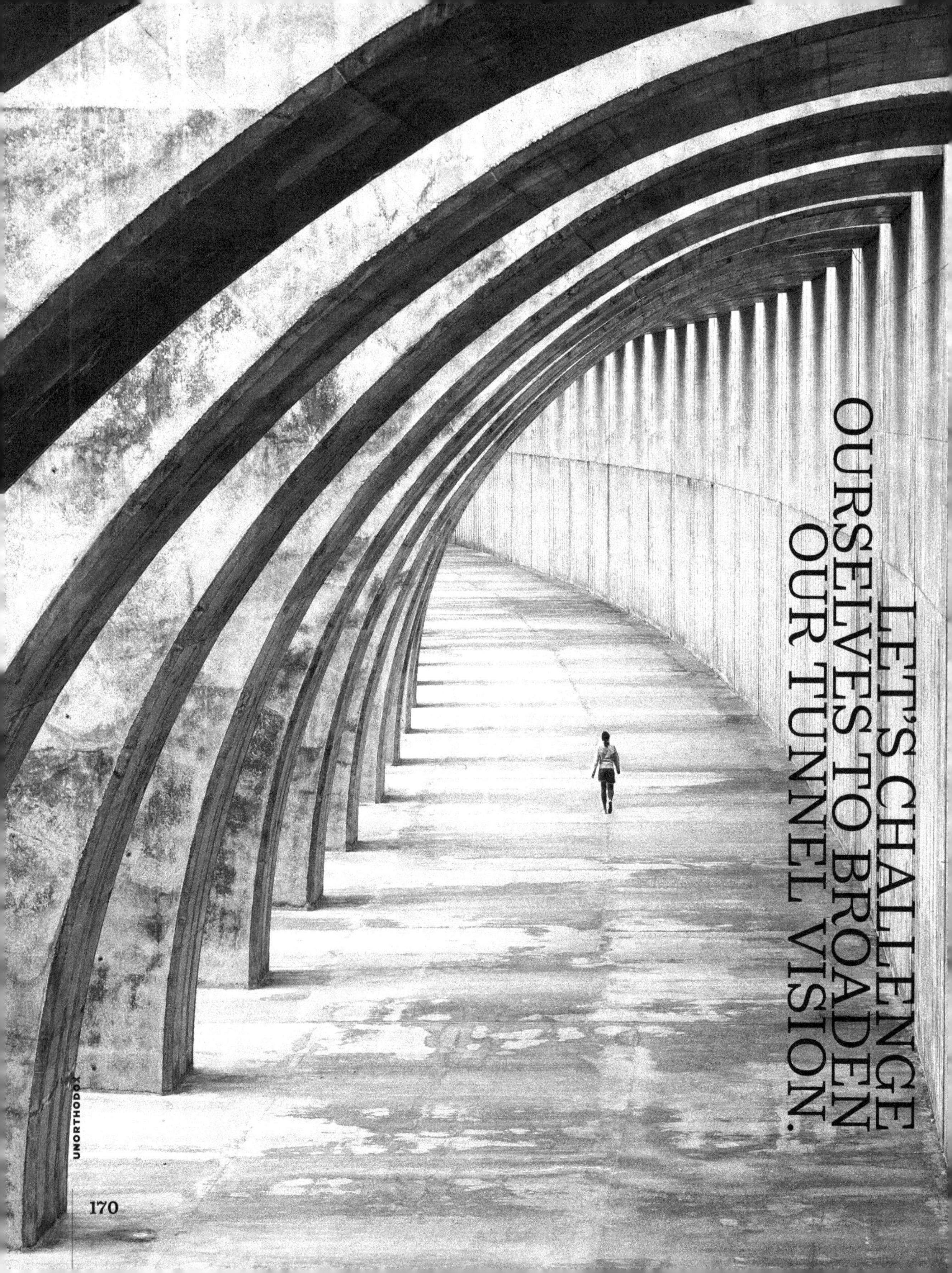

LET'S CHALLENGE OURSELVES TO BROADEN OUR TUNNEL VISION.

JOSEPH

HAD TWO DREAMS that caused him to make a pretty bold move—he decided to share this with his family.

Needless to say, his family was not amused. (That's a bit of an understatement. Their response spoke volumes, wouldn't you say?)

In Joseph's dream, his brothers and parents bowed to who Joseph was destined to become.

As if Joseph wasn't already on his brothers' hit list, he made it to the number one spot!

They envied him and hated him more than ever before!

On the surface, this is not surprising. However, I think it may be worth deeper study and contemplation.

When God gives someone a dream, the manifestation of that dream makes everything else bow.

It's not too difficult to understand why.

Everything bows in the presence of God. Whenever the presence of God manifests throughout the Bible, you see people fall on their faces. When God's dream for your life gets manifested through you, He shows up. As a result, everything in His presence must bow down.

The reality is that dreams are not mutually exclusive. In fact, dreams complement each other.

That's why whenever God gives us a dream, there's no chance of it failing.

Somehow, Joseph's brothers couldn't see the reality that they, too, could have a dream. That they, too, had a prophetic destiny. Because they were blinded to that, they despised and rejected Joseph.

That's what envy does. It causes you to reject the very thing that God has not excluded you from. He doesn't play favorites!

Yet, their assumption was that there could only be one dream.

The reality is that God wants to give dreams and visions to all flesh.

The manifestation of God's dream through you makes me want to bow down the same way His manifestation through my dream will make you want to bow down.

Think about our roadway system. Do all roads begin in the same place, end in the same place, and run parallel to each other? Isn't that absurd to even entertain?

Despite the hyperbolic example, the timing of God's plans to activate our dreams works much the same way. The human race would get nowhere in a highway system of copycat dreams. Be encouraged that your road will get many travelers from point A to point B (including you)—it's just not yet time for the turn.

So, let's challenge ourselves to broaden our tunnel vision. The birth and fruition of our dreams cannot grow and move at the same time. You are not on the same track as your friend, as your brother, or even as your spouse. Don't allow comparison to limit what God can and is going to do.

ACCEPTING

A MEDIOCRE

REALITY

IN

NUMBERS 14:33 (NIV), God told the Israelites, "Your children will be shepherds here for forty years, suffering for your unfaithfulness, until the last of your bodies lies in the wilderness."

Do you ever wish you could avoid the arduous treks in the wilderness? Skip ahead to the good part? Sounds nice, doesn't it?

Before we move forward, let's establish something I think we can all agree on.

You cannot and will not avoid the wilderness (at least, not if you choose the road less traveled).

But you CAN choose how you travel through it and, to an extent, shorten your stay!

A generation refused to cross the river Jordan, causing God's people to wander in the wilderness for forty extra years. This portion of scripture refers to those twenty years or younger at the time. Not by choice but by circumstance, a whole generation had to suffer because of the unfaithfulness of the older generation.

As a result, they were caused to become shepherds in the wilderness.

Let that sink in for a moment. Because of the decisions of others—the decisions their fathers made—the next generation became something they were never supposed to be. This wasn't for a short while, as they were going through a "life transition."

Not even close!

For forty long years, they lived a life they were never supposed to live.

Let's stand in their shoes for a moment. Imagine a world where you see people all around you taking their hopes and dreams into their graves. You, yourself, are settling for a life on the wrong side of the river, unfulfilled and untrue to who you were really created to be. Over an extended period of time, this will break your spirit.

And maybe even the spirit of others.

Before long, you will accept "the truth" that being a "shepherd in the wilderness" is simply what life is all about. Slowly but surely, you'll embrace a life of mediocrity.

Your dreams and hopes will slowly die, and it likely won't end with you. The dream-fulfilling decisions you make that don't include courage and God-directed "risk" (or so we sometimes see it) will be like poison to the soul.

We go through religious motions, saying the right things and pretending we're living the life God wants for us because facing the truth is unbearable. It's simply too painful to accept our reality.

What does that reality look like?

It's a reality of feeling perpetually unfulfilled, hating what we do every day, the reality that we're stuck in a rat race, trying to keep up with everyone else around us, and the reality of barely having enough, needing miracle after miracle to survive the wilderness.

Need I say more?

Let's not settle for mediocrity.

You're a river crosser, so dream big and cross it!

YOU CAN-
NOT AND
WILL NOT
AVOID THE
WILDERNESS
(AT LEAST,
NOT IF YOU
CHOOSE THE
ROAD LESS
TRAVELED).

LET'S NOT SETTLE FOR MEDIOCRITY. YOU'RE A RIVER CROSSER, SO DREAM BIG AND CROSS IT!

35

THIRTY FIVE

WHAT HAPPENS WHEN GOD SHOWS UP?

AS I SPEAK to audiences and congregations, and as I talk with people individually, I often ask these questions: "What happens when God shows up in a place? What happens when His glory manifests?"

When you ask a question like that, you get all kinds of answers:

- When God shows up, the blind will see!
- When God shows up, the lame will walk!
- When God shows up, people will get saved!
- When God shows up, bondage will be broken!
- When God shows up, even the dead will be raised!

Even though all those things are true, there is something far more profound that happens in His presence.

What can be more powerful, you ask?

Let's read about it:

> And it shall come to pass afterward
> That I will pour out My Spirit on all flesh;
> Your sons and your daughters shall prophesy,
> Your old men shall dream dreams,
> Your young men shall see visions. —Joel 2:28 (NKJV)

Two things stand out from this portion of scripture:

1. Your old men shall dream dreams.
2. Your young men shall see visions.

Let's meditate on that for a moment.

That old man lost his dream many years ago. He had lost hope a long time ago. But when God shows up, that man will regain hope and dream again.

Wow!

That young man had never had a vision for his life. The world had looked at him with disgust, telling him that he'd never accomplish anything. But when God pours out His Spirit, that young man will receive vision from God!

The advancement of God's kingdom happens through the manifestation of those dreams and that vision.

Your dreams and visions are the gateway to the supernatural move of God—you only need to open it!

As leaders, our primary task is to facilitate an environment in the church where this process can take place. We need to develop a culture and climate where God can simply pour out His Spirit.

A place where He can show up and release dreams and visions to everyone.

That's how we, together, can change the world!

WE NEED TO DEVELOP A CULTURE AND CLIMATE WHERE GOD CAN SIMPLY POUR OUT HIS SPIRIT. A PLACE WHERE HE CAN SHOW UP AND RELEASE DREAMS AND VISIONS TO EVERYONE. THAT'S HOW WE, TOGETHER, CAN CHANGE THE WORLD!

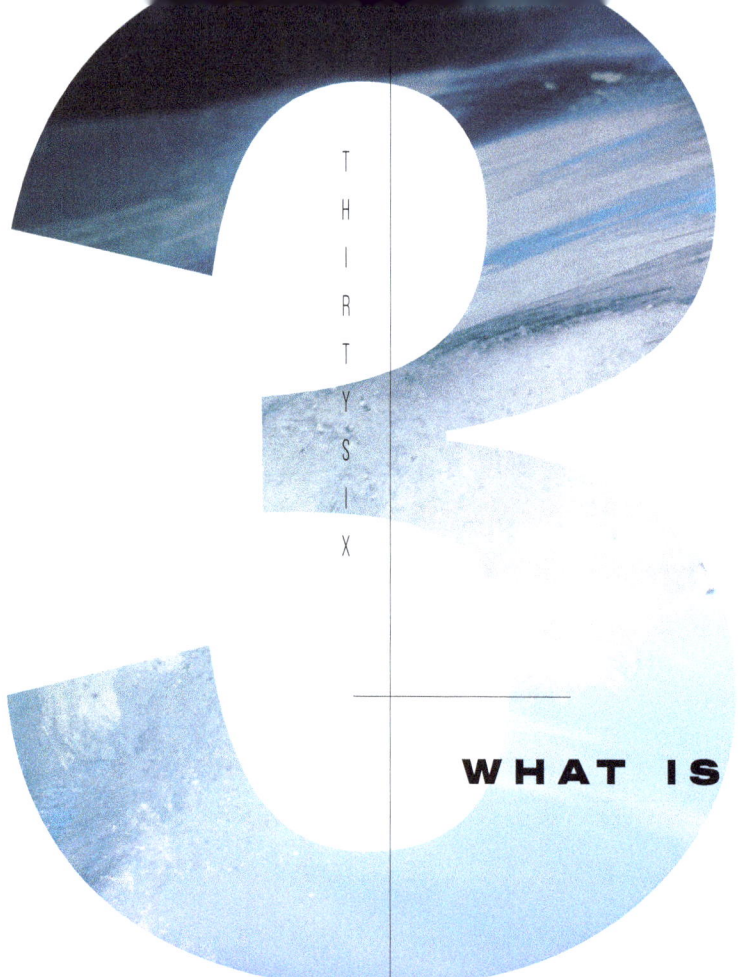

36

WHAT IS THE SHAPE

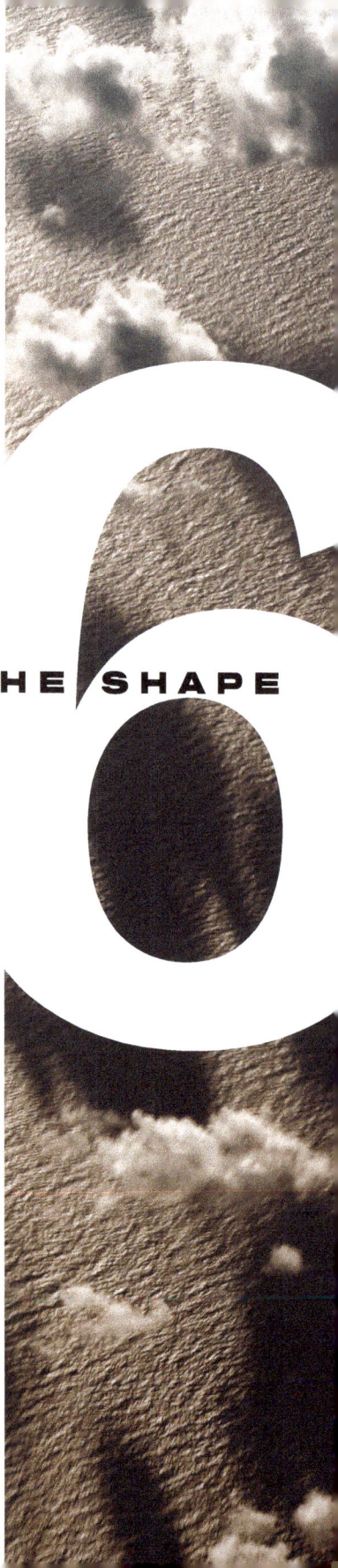

OF WATER?

NO

WATER, NO LIFE, it's that simple. No wonder, then, that there are more than one hundred verses in the Bible that speak of the "living water" that God gives us as believers. It is the greatest asset that He has entrusted us with to bring life to the world around us. So why are so many parts dry and parched?

One reason is that we have inadvertently dammed things up.

One of water's unique properties is that it doesn't have a shape. Left to itself, it can seep into any crack, any space. It will flow to the farthest corners. Its shape is determined by its container. In fact, water cannot take on any other shape than that of what is holding it.

We need to ask ourselves if this might be why God's living water has not reached parts of the world where it is so desperately needed. Could it be that, as church leaders, we have created systems and structures that have become containers limiting its spread; therefore, it can only exist within the shape of our organizations?

Consider that some of the cities in our country with the highest number of churches per capita also seem to struggle the most with poverty, crime, and violence. Somehow, our greatest asset isn't able to pour into the cracks of society and fix our most basic problems.

In the business world, both liquid and nonliquid assets can have tremendous value. However, the full value of a nonliquid asset is not accessible if we want to use it now. Perhaps in many of our churches, we have unwittingly turned our greatest asset—living water—into a nonliquid asset, keeping it from being exchanged in the open market.

I believe we often limit the shape of the living water we've been entrusted with to the four walls of our ministries simply because of some wrong assumptions. If we are to "liquidize" this great asset so that we can truly touch culture and impact our society, we will need to unlearn some basic "truths" that keep us from being effective.

First, we need to look at the world differently!

We don't need another new church program or project to "reach the world." All we need to do is tear down the walls that limit the shape of water and allow it to flow into places where it experiences the least resistance.

Let's be liquid leaders and believers; let's undam our greatest asset and help show how God's people are supposed to be conduits of His living water beyond the church in their everyday lives.

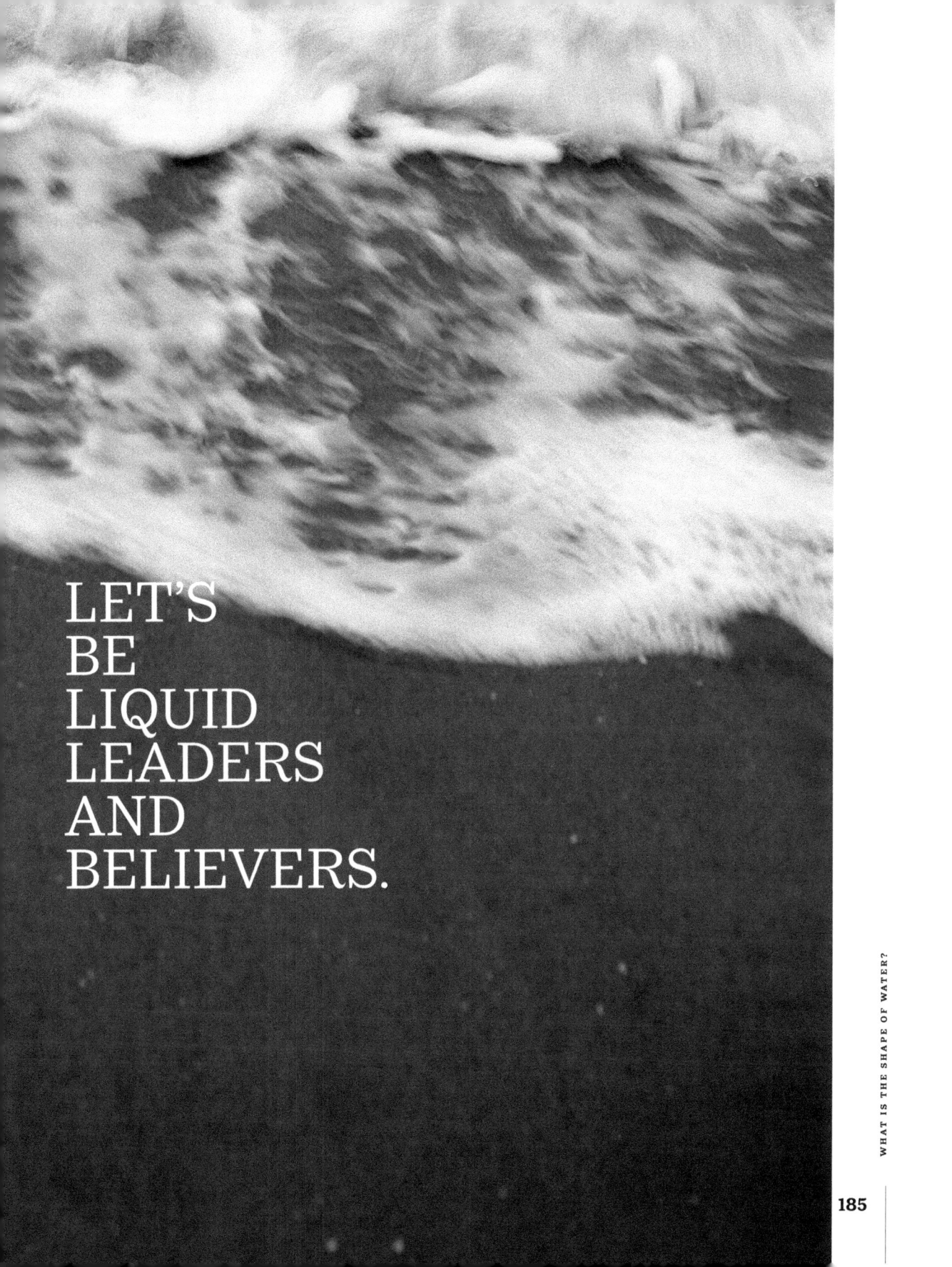

LET'S BE LIQUID LEADERS AND BELIEVERS.

THIRTY SEVEN

3

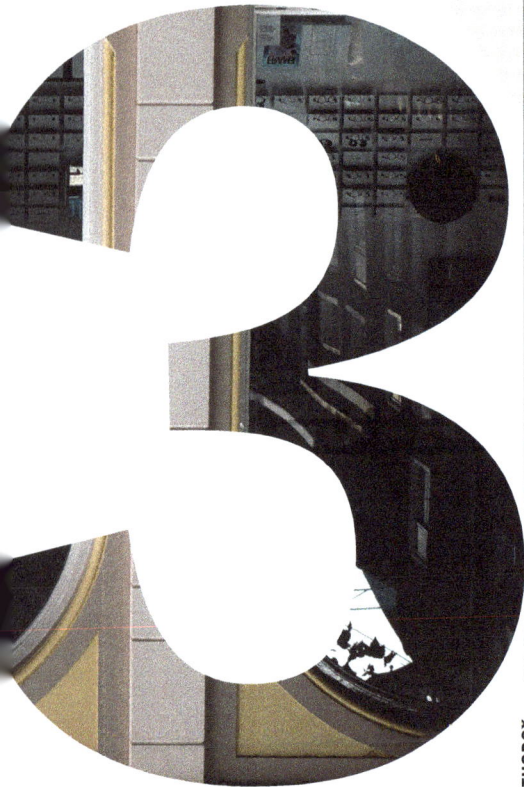

CONFUSION BECOMES YOUR BOUNTY

LOOK
LOOK
LOOK

JOSEPH HAD a dream—one so big (not to mention insulting) that even his own family ridiculed him. His brothers actually despised him because his dream didn't fit the picture they had painted of their future. They weren't too keen on accepting that the brother they detested the most was also going to be a ruler over them.

Talk about stacking resentment upon resentment! Could you imagine receiving that news? This isn't too groundbreaking, but I'm pretty sure we'd throw a fit, too (but maybe not try to kill him).

So, we can put ourselves in the shoes of his brothers, as grotesque as their actions may have been. The fierce rejection they felt led them to sell him off as a slave.

Now, cut to Joseph.

How confusing this must have been for him.

God had made Joseph's vision—brought to him through a dream—burn in his heart. Joseph was a faithful man of God, so he wasn't exactly one to question Him.

Yet, we have to remember that Joseph was still a man, aware of his narrow ways of thinking, aware of his shortcomings, aware of his . . . well, humanness. We don't really need biblical evidence of Joseph's inner dialogue. All we need to know is that he was human, and even the most faithful man doubts. Often, it's not God we are doubting—it's us.

To add insult to injury, the more he shared the dream with those closest to him, the more friction it produced. The discrepancy between his current reality and what he believed was his future destiny must have left him wondering.

Had he been wrong all along?

Yet, in hindsight, years later, it all made sense to him. After Joseph was reunited with his brothers, he put the pieces of the puzzle together and told them: "So then, it was not you who sent me here, but God. He made me father to Pharaoh, lord of his entire household and ruler of all Egypt" (Genesis 45:8, NIV).

It turned out that the prophetic destiny God had declared over Joseph's life could only manifest away from his traditional family setting.

I want to add a little bonus takeaway here—God exceeded the dream he gave Joseph. Not only did his persecutors yield to Joseph's leadership, but He did something much bigger—He restored the family.

Keep this in mind as you traverse through your own disparity. God isn't satisfied with just fulfilling your dream. He has to show off.

In the meantime, maybe you feel like Joseph did: confused, wondering whether or not the dreams in your heart were truly placed there by God. Frustrated because you can't seem to find a way to manifest your vision in your traditional surroundings.

Could it be that God is "sending you to Egypt" in order to manifest your dreams?

Is it possible that God is sending you to become father to Pharaoh, as Joseph did?

CONFUSION BECOMES YOUR BOUNTY

COULD IT BE THAT GOD IS "SENDING YOU TO EGYPT" IN ORDER TO MANIFEST YOUR DREAMS? IS IT POSSIBLE THAT GOD IS SENDING YOU TO BECOME FATHER TO PHARAOH, AS JOSEPH DID?

38

NO MORE EXCUSES!

THERE'S A difference between earning and living up to the standard of God's calling.

God doesn't require a strenuous, arduous, performance-based life to do amazing things (in fact, He wants us to keep that nailed to the cross where it belongs).

We are pleasing before God without an Olympic-esque life. He doesn't need our blood, sweat, and tears before we earn His favor.

BUT, God's freely-given favor isn't a get-out-of-jail-free card. In fact, it's God's grace, mercy, and favor that should propel us to live a life playing big, not small. A life outside of the box that makes waves.

He isn't looking for imperceptible ripples in a pond.

Of course, the waves of our lives roar because of the power He deposits within us to make them.

It certainly has NOTHING to do with us!

I can think of no better example than Jesus Himself.

Before Jesus did anything of significance, before His ministry started, before He healed the sick, cast out demons, and raised the dead, His Dad approved of him.

While this truth has been life-changing for me and many others, I also believe that, too often, we have allowed it to become an excuse for "lack of performance."

God the Father approved of Jesus before He did anything as it relates to public ministry. The Father was "well pleased" with someone who had done "nothing" to prove His "worth" on the day that John baptized Him.

And yet, the story didn't end there. Jesus didn't take the Father's words and use them as an excuse to "sit back and relax."

He took them and used them as fuel to become everything He could possibly become.

He harnessed the love and acceptance of His Father and actually changed the world—forever!

Don't take Jesus's words in John 14:12 (NIV) lightly:

"Very truly I tell you, whoever believes in me will do the works I have been doing, and they will do even greater things than these because I am going to the Father."

That's pretty hard to fathom, isn't it?

What kind of message are we sending to the world by neglecting this responsibility?

And you and I have the same ability and responsibility. Your success is within arm's reach—right at your fingertips.

Let's get off our couches and go trailblaze the path that only WE can pave!

"VERY TRULY I TELL YOU, WHOEVER BELIEVES IN ME WILL DO THE WORKS I HAVE BEEN DOING, AND THEY WILL DO EVEN GREATER THINGS THAN THESE BECAUSE I AM GO-ING TO THE FATHER."

LET'S GET OFF OUR COUCHES AND GO TRAILBLAZE THE PATH THAT ONLY WE CAN PAVE!

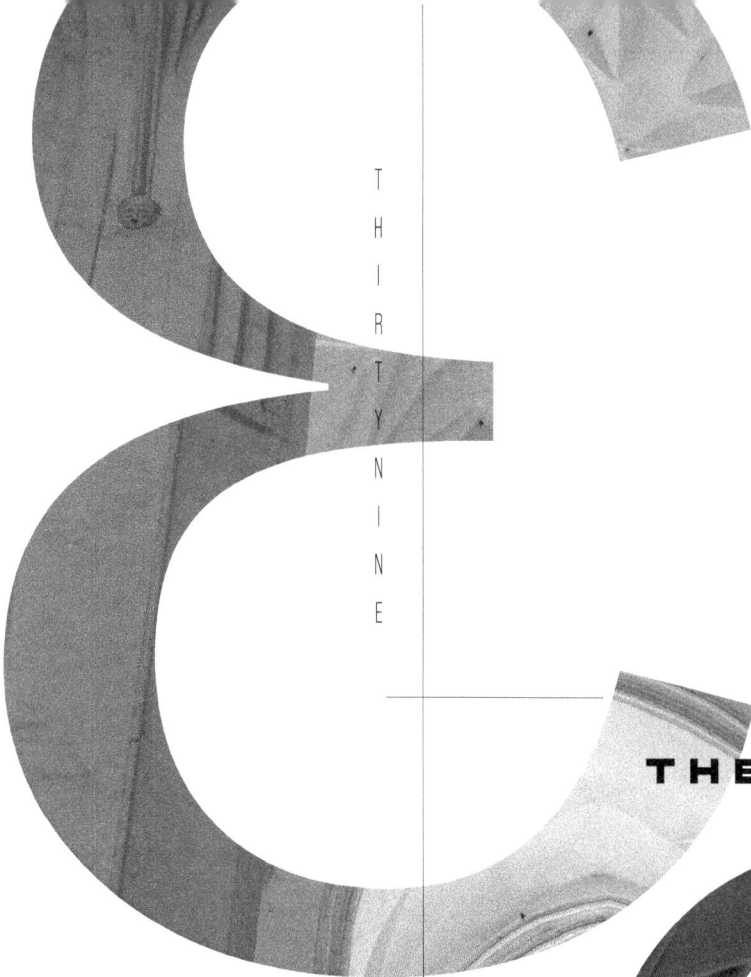

THE SONG THAT

CHANGES EVERYTHING

199

IF YOU'RE really quiet, you can almost hear it.

The sound of a song. A song of celebration. A song of victory. A melody that declares the future as it pushes us away from the past, separating us from what once was but can no longer be.

Once you notice this sound, it cannot be unheard. In fact, its volume will amplify as it becomes stronger and stronger in our ears and hearts as it seeks to manifest the future in our now.

As leaders, not only do we need to recognize the sound of the song, prophetically discern the times we live in, and embrace the changes that the future demands from us, but we need to actually DO something about it.

It's not enough just to hear it, know it, see it, taste it, smell it, and open your heart to it. The song of change requires action!

Consider James's sentiment:

"If one of you says to them, 'Go in peace; keep warm and well fed,' but does nothing about their physical needs, what good is it? In the same way, faith by itself, if it is not accompanied by action, is dead" (2:16-17, NIV).

Discerning and embracing the new melodies that invade your spirit covers the "faith" part, but are you responding to God's call by living in faith without action?

Here's an even greater challenge I'd like

to submit to you.

Is living by faith without the actions that back it up really faith at all?

Pretty sobering and confronting, huh?

I understand that action is often the hardest part of tuning our frequency to the new songs playing in our hearts. It takes courage. Stamina. Grit. Obedience. Patience.

You name it. That's a whole other book in and of itself.

Let this truth become your motto: if God is the author of the song, then it will be a #1 hit.

God is a Hall-of-Famer, and He doesn't want to be inducted without you.

So, the moral of the story is that you are safe to move. There is no greater place of safety than to go where God is leading you. It doesn't matter whether it makes sense or not.

God isn't usually one for logic. I don't know if you've noticed, but He's a bit of a rebel.

He has given you full permission to be a rebel alongside Him. Contrary to the old moniker, "A rebel without a cause," you will be a rebel with a cause!

Don't just listen to the song—sing it!

SECOND BEST

IS NOT YOUR BEST

I THINK sometimes we don't believe we can come out on top. I'm not talking about jockeying for a position above others. I'm talking about undershooting what God has deposited within us and, therefore, underperforming.

We have to wake up from our slumber because the irrevocable, undeniable truth is that there is NO such thing as second best in the kingdom of God.

Yet most of us live as if there aren't enough first-place winners to go around. Like God doesn't have enough room or something.

How ridiculous does that sound?

Scarcity is an illusion. We don't have to stay small and watch others grow big. (Note that this is different from taking the low position to edify others. First-best people can still do that.)

So why is it that we so easily settle for second best?

Why does it seem natural to be okay with our current reality while God says, "No! What I have is so much better!"?

The mind has a unique ability to play tricks on us. Your mind has the power to make you believe that your current state of life is acceptable, even though you know better. You have just become an expert in manipulating your own mind to excuse yourself from aiming higher.

The mind is more powerful than we give it credit for. We are absurdly susceptible to self-delusion. It's a form of self-protection from danger.

The problem is this: living a second-best life is far more dangerous than playing it safe.

Second best is the birthplace of every nightmare you could imagine. Yet, we welcome it with open arms.

Remember the story of the Israelites approaching the river Jordan? They were about to experience the promise God had spoken about their entire lives. It was a pivotal time. The Israelites had the chance to transition from "just enough" into the full manifestation of everything God had for them.

The tragic part of this story is that a full generation of believers accepted the lie that God's destiny for them was, in fact, not for them.

See what I mean by second best as the birthplace of nightmares?

A whole generation of people couldn't bring themselves to receive the greatest miracle they would ever see from God. They settled for second best and died dreamless, empty, and hopeless.

Second best is not your best. Don't accept it.

WE HAVE TO WAKE UP FROM OUR SLUMBER BECAUSE THE IRREVOCABLE, UNDENIABLE TRUTH IS THAT THERE IS NO SUCH THING AS SECOND BEST IN THE KINGDOM OF GOD.

SECOND BEST IS NOT YOUR BEST.

SECOND BEST IS NOT YOUR BEST. DON'T ACCEPT IT.

PHOTO CREDITS

Alphabetical order.

Adrien Converse

Alessio Rinella

Alex Wong

Alexander Andrews

Andrew van Tilborgh

Ben White

Brad Starkey

Brandon Mowinkel

Cathy Mu

Dan Cristian

Daniel Burka

Daniel Splisser

Dave Hoefler

Dhruv

Drew Beamer

Evgeni Tcherkasski

Felix Dubois Robert

Gabriella Clare Marino

Jamie Street

Jayden So

Joel Filipe

John Towner

Michael Dziedzic

Mitya Ivanov

Mohamed Lammah

Peter Herrmann

Ravi Sharma

Reinaldo Kevin

Resource Database

Rihards Dicis

Rodrigo Gonzalez

Seif Amr

Steve Johnson

Taylor Van Riper

Tijs van Leur

Tim Marshall

Travis Essinger

Warion Taipei

www.ingramcontent.com/pod-product-compliance
Lightning Source LLC
Chambersburg PA
CBHW061235150426

42812CB00055BA/2594